THE HORRORS OF THE HOUSE OF WILLS

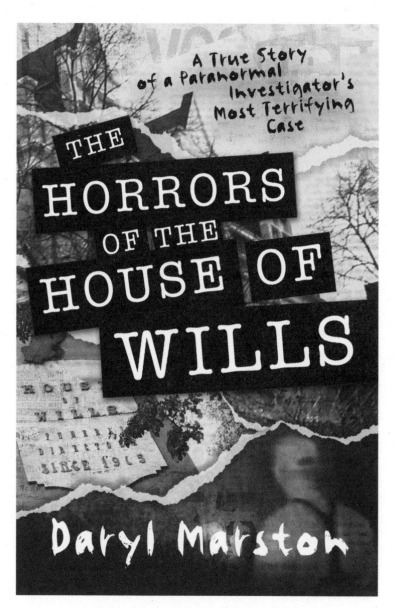

A True Story
of a Paranormal
Investigator's
Most Terrifying
Case

THE

HORRORS
OF THE
HOUSE OF
WILLS

Daryl Marston

Llewellyn Publications | Woodbury, Minnesota

FIRST EDITION
First Printing, 2023

Book design by R. Brasington
Cover design by Shannon McKuhen
Cover photos provided by Daryl Marston
Editing by Marjorie Otto
Interior illustrations by Llewellyn Art Department
Interior photos provided by Daryl Marston

Photography is used for illustrative purposes only. The persons depicted may not endorse or represent the book's subject.

Llewellyn Publications is a registered trademark of Llewellyn Worldwide Ltd.

Library of Congress Cataloging-in-Publication Data (Pending)
ISBN: 978-0-7387-7479-4

Llewellyn Worldwide Ltd. does not participate in, endorse, or have any authority or responsibility concerning private business transactions between our authors and the public.

All mail addressed to the author is forwarded but the publisher cannot, unless specifically instructed by the author, give out an address or phone number.

Any internet references contained in this work are current at publication time, but the publisher cannot guarantee that a specific location will continue to be maintained. Please refer to the publisher's website for links to authors' websites and other sources.

Llewellyn Publications
A Division of Llewellyn Worldwide Ltd.
2143 Wooddale Drive
Woodbury, MN 55125-2989
www.llewellyn.com

Printed in the United States of America

About the Author

Daryl Marston is a co-lead investigator on A&E's *Ghost Hunters*. He has led more than 400 paranormal investigations of private homes and historical locations, such as the House of Wills. He hosts the popular podcast *The American Ghost Hunter Show* and co-owns the website Paranormal Warehouse, which reports on paranormal news. Visit him online at www.ParanormalWarehouse.com.

I dedicate this book to my son, Nicholas Elijah Marston: July 12, 1995, to November 14, 2016. You are gone, my son, but never forgotten. I will see you again someday.
Love you, kid!

Contents

Introduction

Every paranormal investigator is asked, "Where's the scariest place you've ever investigated?" There's always one location that gets to you, follows you home, and beckons you to come back, even though the thought of it gives you chills and you've told yourself to not think about it. From the get-go, mine was always Fort Delaware. It was my first investigation and was where I had my first real paranormal experience. It still calls me back. But we all have that one location that shakes an investigator to our core. If it hasn't happened yet, it will, and when it does, it quite possibly can make or break you, if you let it. This location almost broke me, in more ways than one.

I was torn if I should write my story and tell it as it happened. It's been six years since my terrifying night, and I still remember it like it was just hours ago. I buried a lot of my memories of it deep down inside of me. At first, I found it hard to dig those memories up. After several weeks of writing this book, it all started flowing out, all the emotions and feelings I felt that night and for many months after that. I had been asked to write this book for several years by multiple people and the time was never right. Suddenly one night, something just clicked in me, and I started writing and didn't stop for three months. When it comes down to this location, with all that has occurred there over the last ten years, there are no good guys or bad guys in this story. Just different people with different belief systems that all made this place as haunted as it is, in my opinion. All these different types of energies collided in the spot that we call the House of Wills. I think it was meant to be that way, and it's quite possible that we all were predetermined to meet there. In some cosmic way, who knows if this location didn't draw all our different energies there to make it what it is today. It's almost like the House of Wills is a giant lighthouse drawing people closer to shore like a lost ship in the night.

The reason why I wrote this book and why I believe I am qualified to do so is that I spent many years listening to and investigating eyewitness reports from the House of Wills, not to mention my time spent at the actual location and my experiences that followed while at and after leaving the property. I spent thirteen hours in-person investigating the House of Wills, gathering evidence and firsthand accounts of what I witnessed with my team. I compiled what happened, from my perspective, after leaving the building and what continued to occur over a period of one month after the visit.

The story I am about to tell is completely true. It includes eyewitnesses and my own perspective of what led up to, occurred during, and followed the in-person investigation at the House of Wills. Some of what you are about to read in this story may be disturbing.

This is the story of my time spent at the House of Wills.

Chapter 1

Where It All Began

My journey into the world of paranormal investigating began in the fall of 2005 when my mother bought tickets to a local ghost hunt at Fort Delaware for me, herself, and my stepsister. I had never been on a ghost hunt before, and I had never lived through a paranormal experience I couldn't explain. I didn't even know what a ghost hunter was or what they did. Don't get me wrong, I had some interest in the paranormal, but I was also a skeptic, as I still am to this day.

I lived in a haunted house for several years but have no memories of it because we moved when I was six years old. My parents told me stories of unexplained things that happened while we lived in the house. Furniture often moved around on its own and my parents woke up to the contents of a dresser's drawers dumped on the floor multiple times.

I didn't know what to expect when I decided to go on this new paranormal adventure at Fort Delaware. I thought it was going to be like the movies where things fly across a room or people are possessed by evil spirits. Maybe it would just be a bunch of people telling ghost stories while sitting around a campfire. To prepare, I brushed up on ghost hunting TV shows and was ready for the creepy music and cool equipment.

The night finally came for our ghost hunt, and I was rather excited. Fort Delaware is on an island in the middle of the Delaware River, and you have to take a ferry to it. The fort that stands today was originally constructed to defend Philadelphia from the Confederate Navy during the Civil War, but in the first year of the war, the Confederate Navy was completely wiped out and there was no need for the fort anymore. The Union decided to turn it into a prison camp for Confederate soldiers, and most of the soldiers held there were captured at the Battle of Gettysburg. It was quickly nicknamed the "Andersonville of the north," (after the notoriously bad Andersonville, Georgia, Confederate prison camp, Camp Sumter) by the prisoners for good reason.

It was a late afternoon in October when we visited Fort Delaware, so by the time we boarded the ferry it was almost dark out and the island slowly disappeared into the dark of the night. I remember staring across the river from the ferry dock at the island that seemed so ghostly itself. We sat on the upper deck of the ferry for our twenty-minute journey across the two miles of cold open water to the fort. I thought about how those prisoners must have felt as they made their way to the fort, not knowing if they would ever return to their homes in the South. It must have felt like they were in another world being prisoners of war so far away from the South, where some had never left their home states until the war.

When we got to the island, we were met by a park ranger, who was behind the wheel of a large tractor pulling a covered wagon that seated about twenty people. We all piled onto the wagon and took our seats in excitement. We rode in the wagon for what seemed to be about a quarter of a mile. The suspense was starting to kick in and we all waited to see what was in store for us.

As we made our way through the trees, the fort gradually appeared. We all were taken aback by how ominous and big it really was. The pictures did it no justice. Large torches flanked both sides of a bridge that covered a large moat that surrounded the fort on all sides. We were met by another park ranger who walked us across a bridge, over a moat, and into a large sally port with winding stone stairs on one side. We were then led into a large football-field-size courtyard that was surrounded by twenty-foot-high stone walls on all sides. On top of the walls were walkways from which guards watched over the prisoners. The energy and history of this place flooded me with every emotion. We were given a quick history lesson by the park ranger and shown into a rather large room, which the rangers referred to as the Union soldiers'mess hall.

Almost one hundred people had turned out for this event. I was a little shocked that so many people wanted to hear ghost stories, but it was October, and everyone seemed to be in the spirit for scary stuff. We received another history lesson and broke up into smaller groups and headed out. A park ranger asked to see a show of hands of those who were signed up for the history tour. I looked around the room and almost everyone had raised their hands except us and a couple. Then the park ranger asked for everyone to raise their hands if they were at the fort for the ghost hunt. Out of the hundred or so people in the room, only five of us raised our hands. The ranger pointed to an older gentleman on the other side of the room and told us he was our tour guide and resident ghost hunter, in a slightly mocking tone.

Back in 2005, ghost hunting and talking about the paranormal in public was still taboo. People were afraid of being laughed at or shunned for believing in ghosts. A lot has changed since then, thanks in part to TV shows such as *Ghost Hunters*, which paved the way for a new generation of paranormal enthusiasts. Ghost hunting has turned from taboo to Monday morning water cooler talk or a weekend hobby for many. Many people today have a paranormal story to tell, even the skeptics. John was our tour guide, and if it wasn't for him, my career, and this book, would never have happened.

John had us follow him outside to the courtyard and began to explain where we were headed as we walked across the yard to the far corner. I have heard the fort called everything from the "dungeons" to the "catacombs and prison cells." John referred to it as the "power mag," which is from before it was a prison. This area was where the gunpowder was stored and where the armory was located. He told us that today, the powder mag was home to bats and the occasional muskrat from the surrounding marsh on the island.

We made our way down a long, dark, winding corridor. The walls were just wide enough for us to walk single file. We eventually came to a larger room with high ceilings that smelled of musty gunpowder and urine. He told us what we smelled were the remnants of a powder explosion that killed several Union soldiers. The smell of urine was from the prisoners that were kept there. There wasn't a designated area to relieve themselves, so they went wherever. He explained that human urine is very acidic, and it seeped into the brick and stone walls. The smell as been there since the fort was a prison and most likely will never go away.

John asked us to gather around as he started to tell us about his experiences in the powder mag. As we all stood in a semicircle to listen to John's stories, I saw something in my peripheral vision. As I turned to look in the direction of the movement, I was shocked to see a man standing in the hallway staring at me. I then noticed the man had no lower half. All that was visible of the man was his shoulders and head. He was gray in color with shoulder-length hair and a scraggly, dirty beard full of debris. At first, I thought it might be a reenactor or another tour guide, but the fact there was nothing from the shoulders down was not possible. I watched him for what seemed like minutes but was only about ten seconds. Then, it looked like he was sucked backward into a hole in the middle of the room, and he disappeared. I stood there quietly, in shock, and stared into the room, hoping to get another glimpse of him. I said nothing at the time it happened because I thought the others would think I was making it up or that I was crazy. The man's face I saw that night has been etched into my memory. I can still describe him in detail as if it only happened moments ago. I was excited and confused all at once during the ferry ride back to the mainland. I was excited that I had a paranormal experience but also confused. Why did this man, who was obviously a Confederate prisoner of war, show himself to me, of all people? Was he some distant relative that was imprisoned there and tried to contact me? Or was I in the right place at the right time? When I got home, I lay in bed for hours and still saw the man's face and the expression of sorrow and defeat on it. I could tell he was in a bad way, and he did not want to be there anymore. It saddened me to the core. I had little paranormal things here and there that had happened over the years, but it was very easy to explain or rationalize them. However, there was no dismissing this man I saw at the fort. I saw him as plain as day twenty feet away from me. I knew from this point I was going to do my best to figure out what I experienced and why he chose me to show himself to.

That was my first real paranormal experience, and it felt like finding the holy grail of the paranormal. Not to mention it was my first ghost hunt and I had an amazing experience that piqued my interest to a whole new level. All I knew from that point on was that I was hooked and had to figure all this out. I woke up the next morning with a newfound look at life. I knew nothing about how to investigate or use the equipment, but I did know one thing that night when I left: someway and somehow, I was going to pursue this as my new hobby. I now had a mission to research and educate myself on the field of the paranormal, learn the techniques and how to use the equipment, and find places to investigate. I had no experience in hunting or investigating haunted locations, and it was all new to me, much like starting a new job where you know nothing about the job or any of your co-workers. I had no one to partner with or mentor me it. It was just me and my desire to take on something new that intrigued me.

I started to research and read articles and went down the rabbit hole of the internet. Keep in mind this was 2005 and read random paranormal stories and saw pictures and videos that people had uploaded. I almost believed everything I saw. I will come across some of those pictures and videos now and just laugh at how naive I was back then. These days you can't believe anything that you see online or on any of the social media platforms. In 2005, we did not have social media with all the different types of filters that can be used to create different effects that can fool people into seeing something that is not real. It makes it hard to take anyone's stories or paranormal evidence seriously when it's uploaded for the world to see. You almost need a degree in cinematography to weed out the fakes, since it's hard with the ever-changing world of technology.

I frequented every bookstore in my area to find books on the paranormal and any type of literature or videos I could get my hands on. I started watching the TV shows about ghost hunting that were on at the time. I found the world of paranormal investigations exciting and interesting, and I loved the fact that sometimes they found nothing at all while investigating. That felt real and more believable given that I had gone most of my life without any type of experience at all until that one night.

As many of us did back in the day, I made the mistake of using the TV shows of the time to make my decisions for me. I started collecting whatever new gadget they had at the time, and most of the time I was disappointed in what I purchased and scratched my head over how some of this equipment actually worked or detected spirits. I did find some stuff useful and made the best of it. I started my investigations small and researched top haunted locations in my home state. This was harder than I thought because every time I reached out to a location to see about going there, I wouldn't get a response, or they had no contact information at all.

After several months of trying to find my first location to investigate, I was almost to the point of giving up when someone suggested a place called Crybaby Bridge in Delaware. I look back at this now and cringe because there is literally a crybaby bridge in every state—some actually have more than one—but being a rookie investigator and having absolutely no luck on landing a location, I jumped on it. Plus, it was free and open to the public. Without knowing a whole lot about the location, I went on my first ghost hunt by myself due to the fact I did not know anyone else who was into the paranormal at the time.

The bridge wasn't even on a map. I got directions off a local website and went with it. After several hours of driving the back roads in lower Delaware in the middle of the night, I finally came across what looked to be the bridge. To this day, I'm still not sure if it was even the actual spot or not. Regardless, I parked my car on the side of the desolate road in the middle of nowhere and began my walk to the bridge about a hundred yards away. I remember walking up to the bridge on that cold February night with high anxiety and the hope of experiencing what happened to me at the fort back in October. After I reached the bridge, I thought, What now? Do I just stand here and ask random questions out loud, or should I ask for a certain person that allegedly passed away there?

In the little bit of research I did prior to my visit, there were no names attached to the bridge. There was only a backstory with no real evidence or records it ever happened. It was all folklore at this point, with no real grounds for any of it. The story I read online stated a woman and her child had driven off the bridge one snowy night back in the 1970s and drowned in the river below. When I looked over the side of the bridge, there lay my first clue it was all just a story. There was no river at all. It was a small stream you could step over without getting your shoes wet. I got my first taste of how stories can be diluted over the years of being passed down from person to person. Even though I was disappointed, I knew I had to try to make contact while I was there. Even though there was no raging river under the bridge doesn't mean some poor woman and her child did not drive over it and perish below.

The story I read said people who stop there can sometimes hear what sounds like a baby crying or a woman screaming. The first thing that popped into my head was that in the country, sometimes at night you will hear a fox screaming. It sounds a lot like a woman or a child screaming and will send a chill up your spine and make a person believe the worst is happening to some poor person in the woods. With that in the back of my mind, I decided to try an electronic voice phenomenon (EVP) session. This was my first time using the recorder and I was not that familiar with it. With much fumbling around in the dark, I finally figured it out and began to record my questions for the spirits that were rumored to be there. My questioning process was much like watching a 1950s black-and-white detective show where some poor person is being interrogated under a bright light with some three-piece-suit-wearing, chain-smoking detective grilling them for answers. I look back on it and laugh at how green and inexperienced I was at the time and how far I have come since that night.

After spending close to an hour on the bridge and exploring the area, I noticed how cold it was and decided to end my EVP session and head back to the car. Once I arrived back at the car, I listened to my recorder to see if I caught anything while I waited for the engine to warm up. I sat there listening to myself ramble on and the sounds of the trees and rustling high grass in the cold night and decided to stop the recording and finish it at home.

In the almost two hours I had been out there, not one car had passed over the bridge. Maybe that was what made this place so spooky and how all this folklore began. Almost every small town has its own scary road that the local teenagers swear is haunted, or if you travel that road at a certain time of night you will be attacked by an evil monster looking to sacrifice any unwilling traveler daring to go down it late at night. We had our own place just like that called Devil's Road. My high school friends and I would go out there on Friday nights and try to scare one another and any poor kid that decided to hang out with us.

After I arrived back home, I sat down and listened to the rest of the recording. By the time I reached the end, I was disappointed I had not heard any voices besides my own, but I was not discouraged. I was new to this and knew it would take time for me to learn and master my skills. But quite honestly, in this business there are no masters or experts. You're constantly learning new things and trying to better yourself.

Fast-forward a few years later. I investigated every local haunt I could gain access to. I started dating my now-wife Melanie in late 2008, and she had always been interested in the paranormal but had never ventured to a haunted location. We hit the road every other weekend and tried to find new haunted places to check out. One of our favorite spots was Gettysburg, Pennsylvania, where we had many interesting experiences and captured a lot of paranormal activity, such as EVPs and pictures that were unexplainable. We stayed in almost every bed and breakfast in the area at one point or another. One of our favorite places to stay was the Cashtown Inn, not just for its paranormal activity, but also its history and beauty. One time we rented one whole floor to ourselves for five days and brought my mother and my oldest son, Nicholas, along. Between investigating and holding down a busy family life with work and kids, we went to other locations like Moundsville, West Virginia's state penitentiary, and Hinsdale House. We helped local teams on their investigations and helped local homeowners with whatever paranormal activity was going on in their properties. Times were fun and we met new people all the time who were just like us. In return, we built a network of connections that I still use to this very day.

In 2011, I started my own team, which I named Breaking Paranormal. I wanted to expand, explore larger locations and travel farther into other states. I teamed up with Stephanie and Greg, who were from Akron, Ohio, whom had I met on social media, and Keith, a friend I'd known for years. We spent a lot of time meeting up to investigate some of the East Coast's most haunted locations, such as Eastern States Prison, Anderson Hotel, and the J. C. Thompson building, to name a few. We were always on the lookout for a place to investigate.

Chapter 2

The Calling

In June 2015, I first heard its name mentioned during an investigation around two in the morning in Gettysburg, Pennsylvania. This name runs a chill up my spine to this very day and makes me uneasy when mentioned: the House of Wills. I refer to the House of Wills in Cleveland, Ohio, as a living entity, like many people who fall into its allure and calling. This is the story of the location that broke and humbled me then rebuilt me as a man and a paranormal investigator.

First, we need to go back to November 2014. I had been ghost hunting for about nine years at that point. I thought I had seen everything when it came to the paranormal. I was cocky and immature as an investigator. I thought I was bulletproof and couldn't be harmed or moved by anything. Oh, how I was wrong. During that November, I was posting pictures from a recent investigation on my group's social media page when I received a message from a Stephanie who lived in Canton, Ohio. She said she and her friend had recently left a paranormal group they belonged to and asked about investigating with my team. I live about forty-five minutes south of Philadelphia, so Canton, Ohio, is about eight hours away. I was going to decline Stephanie's suggestion, but then she mentioned she had always wanted to investigate Gettysburg. Slam on the brakes, that spot is right up my alley. At that point in 2014, my wife, Melanie, and I had investigated Gettysburg more times than I can possibly remember, and I was always up for the two-hour road trip to my favorite haunted town.

Fast-forward to June 2015. After eight months of group chats, phone conversations, and text messages, we finally met up at Gettysburg, every paranormal investigator's dream location. Stephanie, her friend Greg, my wife Melanie, team member Keith, and I spent about nine hours jumping from spot to spot, investigating anywhere we could. And then it happened like a shot in the dark when everything changed and life was never the same. Stephanie and Greg pulled me aside like it was some top-secret mission and said I needed to come to Cleveland to investigate this place called the House of Wills.

I had never heard of the House of Wills or been to Cleveland, so when Greg brought up the name to me, it did not ring a bell. However, the name itself captivated me for some reason. I asked Greg what was so great about this place, and his reply was that it was too good to be true. He said it was a paranormal investigator's dream, a place full of shadow figures, amazing EVPs, and everything in between. Not long into the conversation, Melanie and Keith walked over and started asking questions about the location and its back-story, but I didn't need to hear anymore. I was sold and was going to find a way to get there.

After I left Gettysburg, I could not shake the House of Wills. I knew I had to go to Cleveland. I couldn't stop thinking and dreaming about the location and I hadn't even seen a picture of it yet. However, due to vivid and detailed dreams, I knew what almost every room in the building looked like down to the decaying wallpaper and carpets. I knew what it smelled like and the taste in the air when you entered the building. My wife, Melanie, thought I was going crazy with all my talk about this place we hadn't set foot in. I needed to visit this location. Roughly three weeks later, I was finally going to the House of Wills.

Chapter 3

The History

Our trip came together quickly, and the investigation itself was going to be a brief one. It is an eight-hour drive from my house to Cleveland. We planned to conduct a thirteen-hour investigation at the location, and then drive the eight hours straight back to Delaware so I could be at work on Monday morning. That's right, you read me correctly: all that in less than two days. Melanie was smart and said, "Hell no" when I asked her if she wanted to go on the investigation. There was no way she was going to make that trip in such a short time. Not to worry: I had Keith, my trusty sidekick-investigator friend and team member to accompany me.

I personally don't like knowing a whole lot about a location before I get there. I feel as if it may sway my way of collecting evidence or the way I approach the investigation.

For example, my team and I once investigated a location called the J. C. Thompson Building in East Liverpool, Ohio. We knew very little about the history of the location beyond it being a speakeasy in the 1920s and 1930s and the fact that there had been several deaths on the property over the last hundred years or so. At one point during that investigation, we captured an EVP that mentioned the phrase "axe murderer." With the recording in hand, we approached the owner of the building and played the recording we captured. The woman who owned the location had lived in that town her entire life, so she knew the history well. When she listened to the EVP we caught, she was dumbfounded because there were two unsolved crimes in the 1970s that happened on the same block where the building was located. What supposedly happened was a woman was murdered in her sleep with a blunt object the police believed to be either an axe or hatchet. Five years later, on the same block, a husband and wife were found murdered the exact same way with what the police believed to also be a blunt object such as a dull axe or hatchet.

My point in sharing this story is that we were never given this information prior to our investigation because it was kind of a sore spot in the history of the town and mostly forgotten, until we got that amazing EVP and were able to correlate what actually happened. I'm not saying a ghost or a spirit told us about some unsolved crime, but it's pretty interesting and coincidental that we got that recording. This is why I prefer not knowing too much about a location before investigating it. On the show *Ghost Hunters,* we had to know everything about a location before filming and were always sent a packet weeks in advance that gave a complete rundown of the history of the location and accounts from eyewitnesses and the clients.

Even though I didn't research the history of the location before I set foot in the House of Wills, I will give a quick history of the location to give some context of the building before getting into the story of my experience.

The history of the House of Wills is a shadowed one, indeed. I have heard many variations of its birth. Quite honestly, I am not sure if I believe any of them to be accurate since there's so much folklore surrounding the place, so I will give you a variation of both what I have been told and what I researched online in the Cleveland archives.

The location that we all know as the House of Wills was not actually called that until 1941, when J. Walter Wills Sr. took ownership of the building. The location was originally known as Gesangverein Hall and was built in 1898 as a German dance hall for the local community at the time. The year the building was constructed is one of many unknowns.

The architect of this building was Frederic William Striebinger. He was born on April 22, 1870, and was a local architect with a list, as long as my arm, of accolades and honors from the city of Cleveland. Besides being an accomplished architect, he was a well-known member of the Scottish Rite Masons and the Knights Templar. Those affiliations brought great honor to him and his family as a businessman in the city at that time. He also was the architect of several other Masonic temples and Christian Science churches in and around Cleveland. Striebinger died on September 30, 1941. He was well recognized for his accomplishments by his family and peers, and many of the thirty-one buildings he was known to have designed are still standing in Cleveland to this very day. I was not able to find anything in the archives to say to what degree of mason Striebinger was, but seeing his list of accomplishments, I don't doubt one bit if he was not a 33-Degree mason and possibly a Sovereign Grand Commander with his standing in the community.

Over the years, I have often been asked how many rooms are in the House of Wills. Quite honestly, I can't really answer that question. I always say there were too many for me to count or remember. With a little research, I was able to find out there were forty-two rooms when the building was constructed. That's not to say that in its over one hundred-year history some were not added or taken away under the different owners. Whatever the number is today, believe me, it's a lot of rooms.

Gesangverein Hall, the German social club, lasted for about fourteen years until it shut its doors. After that, the building became a hospital for Hungarian immigrants. This lasted until 1920, when it became the home of the Cleveland Hebrew Institute. The institute kept its doors open for eighteen years until the property was bought in 1941 by J. Walter Wills Sr. and became known as the House of Wills.

During this time, it was the largest African American funeral home in Cleveland.

I was told the building was rumored to have housed a speakeasy during Prohibition, but I was not able to find any evidence to confirm the rumor. Speakeasies were supposed to be secret locations that only certain people knew about. It is possible it was a speakeasy and was never recorded in the Cleveland history books because it was never found.

Mr. Wills was a prominent business owner in East Cleveland, with many years under his belt as a mortician and funeral director. He was well-known as an innovator in the field of mortuary science and funeral procedures and was held in high regard as a businessman in his community. J. Walter Wills Sr. was born in eastern Kentucky in 1874 to parents who were slaves freed after the Civil War ended. He moved to Cleveland, Ohio, in 1899 as a strikebreaker for the Cleveland Street Rail Company. He wanted to pursue a career in medicine and attended night classes until he received his degree. In 1904, he was offered a partnership, for $250, with William Gee, who was a mortician. They started their own funeral home called Gee & Wills that ran until Gee's death in 1907.

THE HOUSE OF WILLS IN CLEVELAND, OHIO

In its heyday, the House of Wills, under J. Walter Wills Sr.'s guidance, conducted up to eight funerals in a single day. Following in his footsteps were his biological son J. Walter Wills Jr. and his adopted son Harry Allen Wills. J. Walter Wills Jr. passed away in 1967, and his father and adopted brother ran the business until 1971. When J. Walter Wills Sr. passed away, he left the business to Harry. The remaining family members ran the business until 2005, when it was forced to close its doors because of malpractice and fraud due to the family collecting money for services that were never provided. It lay vacant until 2010, when Eric Freeman took ownership of the building from the City of Cleveland. He planned to reopen the building as a community center

for the surrounding neighborhood. The building is still cur-
rently under renovation and owned by Eric Freeman. This
building has been home to many kinds of people from different walks of life in its history. Even up to this very day,
with all of its controversy, the House of Wills still stands as
a monument in East Cleveland and is almost untouched by
the ever-growing city around it.

Chapter 4

An Ominous Prelude

The night before we were set to leave on our trip, I decided to go to bed early because I knew we had a long day ahead of us. Melanie was still up since she's a night owl. Around ten at night, my dog Ben started howling and barking so much that I jumped out of bed and grabbed my sidearm from the gun safe on the dresser. I'd never heard him act like this, so I was concerned that someone was trying to break in or was trespassing.

I immediately ran downstairs. Melanie and Ben were staring out the French doors that overlooked the backyard and I asked what the hell was going on. She said in a low and slightly concerned voice that she no idea what he was barking at. Without haste, I approached the doors. Ben, who was at my side, started growling at something while he stared into the darkness. He is a forty-pound basset-beagle mix, so he has a big bark but not a lot behind it. I live in the middle of nowhere on a back road, so add that to the suspense of all of this.

There I am, standing in my underwear, holding my sidearm, with my dog by my side, staring out the back door in the middle of the night. I slowly unlocked the door, opened it even slower, and took a few steps outside. I waited for someone or something to jump out or at least run off, but nothing happened. Ben still stared into the darkness and growled at something that neither I nor Melanie could see. I slowly backed into the house and waited to see if anything came into view. Nothing happened, so I returned to bed and shrugged it off as nothing. It was just a dog being a dog.

I woke up early the next morning and the house was eerily quiet. It was the middle of the summer, yet everything was silent. There were no birds outside chirping, no crickets, and even the clock on the kitchen wall didn't make a noise. I started my coffee and decided to go downstairs to check on everything after the events from several hours before. When I got to the bottom of the steps, Ben was still at the back door and staring into the backyard. He'd never done that before that night or since. He always sleeps in our room or in his crate upstairs, so with a little coaxeing and a dog treat, I was able to get him to come back upstairs. It was a bit unsettling at the time, and I've since learned that animals sense, see, and smell things way before we do. I think Ben could sense what was to come in the very near future, like a prophet that predicts impending doom. He was right about the fact that things were going to get upsetting and scary real soon for all of us. Maybe he was trying to tell me what was waiting in the darkness.

Keith and I hit the road together and headed to parts unknown: Cleveland and the House of Wills. Fast-forward through the long, excruciating drive through Pennsylvania to the Ohio border. Keith and I were pretty excited about this location and all the amazing stories and folklore behind it.

We stopped in Canton, Ohio, to meet Greg and Stephanie at Greg's house and pick up his equipment. Keith and I were pretty tired from our seven-hour drive, but we were getting our second wind at this point because of the excitement of being less than an hour from Cleveland. We got the cars loaded up full of equipment and a gas generator (there was no power at the location). The only room in Greg's car was basically the driver's seat. I am still not sure how he drove a Honda Civic with a generator sticking out the hatchback and hard cases packed to the ceiling. But off we went down a long stretch of highway, with almost every sign saying how many miles we were from Cleveland. Things were starting to get real at this point. Our anxiety got worse the closer we got to the location. Before we knew it, we were in East Cleveland. I know some people are going to say they have more dangerous spots in their hometown. I get it. Every state, city, and town has bad areas. I've traveled all over this great nation of ours and have seen some unsavory spots, but if you have ever been to that part of Cleveland, you can feel it in the air. The tension is real!

Closer and closer we crept down the street toward the place I'd been having vivid dreams of for weeks. I will never forget the first time I saw it standing there, all alone in the middle of East Cleveland, like a medieval gargoyle standing watch over the neighborhood. I turned into a large vacant parking lot that was overgrown with weeds. The blacktop crumbled under our tires as we drove across it.

THE HOUSE OF WILLS PARKING LOT, CRUMBLING AND OVERGROWN WITH WEEDS

It was a smoldering August afternoon and the neighborhood was alive with people on the sidewalks and playing basketball across the street in the housing development. We pulled up in front of this massive decaying structure that looked as if it was lost and forgotten in time. In the same parking lot, I noticed what looked to be a vacant church of some denomination. Keith and I were quiet and stared through the windshield. I'm sure we both thought the same thing: what did we get ourselves into. It was almost as if we were in a trance, staring into the abyss of what was to come.

A knock on the driver's side window startled us out of our trance. It was Stephanie and Greg asking if we were just going to sit there all day or get out. We slowly rose out of the car and felt unsteady, as if we were standing on hallowed ground. Greg explained we had to wait for George, one of the building's caretakers, to bring the keys and open the building. Stephanie said that George was going to let us in the building, and Patty, the other caretaker, was going to swing by later that night to check up on us at some point.

THE LOCKED DOORS LEADING INTO THE HOUSE OF WILLS

As we waited for George to arrive, I happened to notice something. The streets were full of people, but I didn't see one person walk across this parking lot or even on the sidewalk in front of this building. I must have said it out loud because Greg answered me and said they are afraid of the place. I laughed and said, "What?" Greg began to explain that they believe all the bad things that happen in this neighborhood happen because of this place. I asked, "Why? They say it's evil and it's a curse on all of them." After hearing this, I walked to the sidewalk in front of the building to get a closer look. I watched for several minutes in shock as people crossed the street to avoid walking in front of the building. I had never seen anything like this up to this point in my days investigating and I haven't seen anything since. Just then, I noticed a crowd of people young and old gathering watching us from across the street. I imagine they wondered why we were there and what good we could possibly be up to in that place they feared so much that they wouldn't even walk past it in fear for their lives, and maybe even their souls.

I look back at that moment and I think how smart they must have been compared to us. Because they knew what was ahead for us that hot night in Cleveland once the sun went down.

Chapter 5

The Gathering

George pulled into the parking lot in his work truck from the late 1970s. We all stood there for several moments and waited for him to get out of the truck, but nothing happened. I decided at this point I had driven this far and my patience was growing thin. I was itching, no I was needing to get into the building. It was as if it was my drug of choice and the only thing between me and it was George, who was stopping me from getting my fix. As I think back, that was the start of all it for that night. The building had its hooks in me and I would stop at nothing to get to it.

I started to approach the truck and all of a sudden, the driver's side door flew open. I stopped dead in my tracks as if I was ready for a fight. But then this thin, wiry guy hopped out with phone to ear and kind of gave us the head nod as if to tell us he was sorry for the delay and to give him a moment to finish. You know, the nod of someone who tries to do ten things at once. I've been there; I get it. He looked as if he'd spent most of his adult life on a job site. He talked fast, was very energetic, and you'd have to take a few moments to process what he actually said to you since he was already five steps past what he said to you.

In one breath, he hung up the phone and went into explaining his day and how crazy it had been. I laughed to myself as I looked at Keith, who rolled his eyes and thought what I was thinking: Dude, we just drove eight hours!

After a quick introduction of everyone, George says we need to clear the house before we investigate. What? Did you say clear as in sweep, like what police and military units do to make sure no one is in a location? He said, "Yeah, just like that!" I'm a licensed firearms instructor and train those who want a concealed carry permit. I'm licensed or have reciprocity in over thirty states. Keith is also licensed to carry, so this was right up my alley. I know exactly how to clear a place. George asked if we had his back, and believe me, we were well prepared because I don't leave home without my sidearm.

I asked George why he thought there would be someone in the building, especially when everyone around was afraid of the place. He said every once in a while, someone who is high on drugs or very brave will break in and try to steal copper out of the walls. The last trespasser he knew of got lost or trapped in the building and went crazy. I asked George how he knew the trespasser went crazy. George said we needed to ask Patty about that because she was there when it happened. He tried to kill Patty with an axe.

"Okay, some dude just tried to randomly kill her?" I asked.

George said, "Yeah. Crazy, right? Ask her about it."

"I definitely will," I replied.

George asked if we were ready and I said, "Absolutely! Let's do this."

There was no turning back now. We headed to the side door that led into the back garage area of the building. My anxiety was high and my hands were literally shaking at this point. That's one thing that never happens to me, especially on an investigation. I am always even-keeled no matter what, but this time it was different. As George put the key into the door handle, it was as if time slowed down. The door slowly opened and pushed through some clutter on the floor as if the building had been vacant for years. George looked puzzled, as if something was wrong. He said it was funny and didn't know why anything would be in the way of the door. This was the only entrance and exit they used because everything else was blocked off. The first thing that came to my mind was someone had possibly broken in and knocked some things over and exited another way. I asked George when the last time anyone was in here. He looked at me and told me it was maybe a week ago that he knows of, and only three people have the keys to the property. I suggested he call them and see if they could have done this. He explained it was not possible because they would have to go out another way and they don't do that for security reasons.

We were on high alert. Even George looked a little frazzled at this point, and we hadn't stepped foot into the building. I pulled out my flashlight and said, "Lead the way" to George as my other hand slowly pulled my shirt over my holster for quick access to my sidearm if needed. Tensions were high because we had no idea what layed around every corner of this massive location. Believe me when I say we were expecting someone or something to be in there judging by the look on George's face. As we started our so-called sweep of the building, we came to a set of stairs that went from the garage area we entered into up to the floor above us. To this very day I remember the smell of the building. It was different from what I expected. It was a scent of lavender with a hint of decay. It was a strange combination and something I never thought I would encounter in my life.

As we stood at the bottom of the stairs, we stared into the dark abyss that the stairs led into, with just a shimmer of light from the door we left open behind us. We slowly started to climb the steps into the darkness, with our flashlights directed at every step we took up the creaking staircase. George suddenly stopped and pointed out there were a couple steps missing in the middle of the staircase and it got a bit sketchy. Greg spoke up and said, "Oh yeah, I forgot to tell you that there's a hole in the middle of the staircase." I laughed sarcastically under my breath: "Thanks, bro, for the warning."

We finally made it to the first floor (see page 175). I know what you are thinking. We just went up a flight of steps. Correct! But the way the building was designed, the garage is

A MAZE OF STAIRS

lower than what they call the first floor. This will become clearer later in the story. This place is built like a giant maze and I can understand how you could get lost very easily if you had never been in the place before. I remember walking into the hallway at the top of the stairs and realizing how unsettlingly dark it was in the building. It was still daylight outside since it was July and about six at night at that point. The crazy thing is there were windows in almost every room at this level. The darkness was so oppressive, it was almost as if the light was not able to penetrate it. The feeling of heaviness was almost unbearable. The only way I can explain it is that it felt like when you walk into a room of strangers, you don't know anyone in the room, they all are staring at you, and you feel like they all are judging your every step. You look for the one seat in the room, it's at the far side of the room, and you have to make your way through everyone to take a seat. Well, imagine that in the dark in what you can only explain to people as the most terrifying location you have ever been to on an investigation. That's what it feels like in the House of Wills!

We tried our best to make our way through every room to make sure no one was hiding out with an axe or some other kind of weapon to wreak havoc on one of us. We looked in closets, under furniture—you name it. We looked everywhere. We found nothing at all on the first floor except for the feeling we were being watched by a thousand eyes that didn't want us there.

George asked us where we wanted to go next. Do we keep going up or hit the basement first? I said let's do the basement and work our way up. If we are in the basement, we can hear if someone leaves the building, so down into the darkness we all headed (see page 176).

A MAZE OF STAIRS

The carpet on the stairs looked as if had been there since the 1960s and was covered in debris and the occasional carcass of some poor animal or bird that met its demise in this place. What a horrible way to die, in that building of all places to meet your end, stuck for eternity. No thanks, not me. As we crept slowly down the stairs to the basement, we started to get a musty, damp, decaying smell, almost like formaldehyde. This actually made complete sense because for a long time, the building was the largest funeral home in Cleveland. It just so happened that the basement was where they performed cremations and embalming. This is also where the House of Wills became top news in Cleveland history in the early 2000s when it was shut down by the city and state for malpractice for not living up to and performing its duties as a funeral home. This onetime pillar of the community that was a place of worship where people could rejoice and was full of family values became a place of sorrow, despair, and hatred due to greed and disloyalty.

As we entered through the doorway of the basement, we walked into a huge room that was still decorated as a viewing area for families to spend their last moments with their deceased loved ones. The first thing that entered my mind was how many people once layed here waiting to be transported to their final resting place. Were any of them still here for some reason? Maybe some of the ones that were not actually taken care of properly at the end of this place's days of service were still here and upset.

While I stood in this huge room, I looked to my right and saw my friends walking down a few steps to another area that reminded me of something from a medieval castle, and not like the big room from my previous daydream or what seemed like a vision. At the bottom of those few steps was a small area with several doors, two that I definitely remembered. The first one led to a large room with several bulk-head windows and what looked to be an old turn-of-the-century furnace. I looked past the furnace, and in the dark were several caskets that were used for viewing purposes only before a body was cremated. Yep, that giant furnace was not for heating the place but for cremation. How many bodies layed in those caskets over the years? We slowly and quietly moved back out of the room one at a time. Reality started to kick in as to how morbid and sad it was in the room. We were dealing with real people who once lived and died, and this place was one of their last stops before being put in a grave or being cremated.

I stopped for a moment as George walked up the small flight of steps. I asked where does this other door lead, and he said the subbasement. Wait, what? If it wasn't creepy enough, the basement has a basement. I slowly opened the door and waited for some creature from the depths of hell to pop out. Right then, the overwhelming smell of mold and God only knows what else hit me. I shined my light down the steps and saw everything covered with a thick white mold. The walls, the floor, the stairs, and I mean everything was covered in mold. I immediately started coughing, quickly shut the door, and said, "NOPE! I'm not going down there." George then said, yeah there's mold down there. I sarcastically thanked George for the warning as I coughed up a lung. I made a beeline for the steps to go back upstairs and told everyone to get out of there.

I quickly ran up the steps to the first floor. I felt like I was running for my life from some unseen force. I finally felt as if I could breathe again once I was upstairs. Everyone finally caught up to me at the top of the stairs and was almost laughing at how fast I ran out of there. We all rested for a moment to catch our breath since we were all winded. It was as if none of us had ever climbed steps before.

Off we went to make sure the rest of the building was safe for the night ahead of us. We reached the second floor, and I felt very uncomfortable (see page 174). If you have ever felt true, pure evil, not evil made by man, but true inhuman evil that was never human at any time but has been around since before man, that's the House of Wills. It's the only location out of the hundreds I have had the honor of investigating that felt like the building itself was the entity. Not haunted or possessed, but alive and very, very intelligent, feeding off your fears and any baggage you brought in those doors once you set foot inside.

We were clearing rooms as quickly as I could move us through them due to our feelings of being very uncomfortable on this floor. We came to a point in the hallway where there were double doors on either side of us. I stopped and waited for George to give some kind of direction, but there was nothing but dead silence. I quickly swung my flashlight behind me but no one was there. I swore I heard them coming down the hall, but I had left everyone behind in my haste to get off that floor. I then did a double take. When I had turned my light on to look behind me, I caught a brief glimpse of something that registered in my head. Did I see what I thought I saw? I quickly turned and faced down the hall and shined my light to the end of it. Yes, it's exactly what I thought. The hall was littered with empty coffins that had most likely been there since the day the funeral home shut its doors.

I soon heard the rest of the group approach. I didn't even bother asking what way next. I just grabbed the handles to the doors to my left and swung them open. I was in complete shock over what was on the other side. I slowly stepped forward onto the second-floor balcony of a huge cathedral (see page 174) that encompassed almost the entire side of the building.

THE CATHEDRAL SPACE WITHIN THE HOUSE OF WILLS

THE CATHEDRAL SPACE WITHIN THE HOUSE OF WILLS

Keith and I were both taken aback by its size and how it's hidden inside the building from the outside world and the hundreds of people who drive and walk by the building every day. You honestly would never know it was there or believe it if someone told you unless you saw it with your own eyes. The only light in the room was some beams of sunlight breaking their way through a bank of old windows covered with vines. These windows lined the fifty-foot ceilings over the second-level balconies that wrapped around the entire second level. It was almost like the sun was making its way through the clouds on a dark autumn day. I walked through a row of chairs and peered over the rail to the floor below me to see pews lined up like a Sunday church service but covered with years of dust and fallen debris from the ceiling. It looked like the roof had been leaking and in disrepair for many years. I noticed an area in between some pews where the floor was caved in from the water damage. I saw a large stage area to the front of the room with what looked like white candles littering the stage. I also saw several large statues placed in the middle of the room. From this distance, I couldn't make them out, so I asked George what those statues were for. I could literally hear a pin drop. No one said anything. Then George finally spoke up and said they are the owner's personal collection. He then said, with a strange look on his face, that he didn't agree with them, but he's the boss, and then George walked back toward the double doors. Stephanie and Greg said at almost the same time they would explain later what George meant when no one else was around. They both quickly moved toward the doors and left Keith and I puzzled as to what this was all about. We followed the rest of the group back into the hallway where they had already entered the double doors across the hall.

We entered what looked to be a large industrial-type condo with some old furniture thrown about and a large open casket on the far side of the room as if it was set up to display a corpse during a viewing. This room was different from most of them in that it had large windows that covered the exterior walls of the room. Surprisingly enough, the room was full of late summer sunlight. From this height, you could get a good look at the surrounding city skyline.

I then noticed something on the far side of the room that, to this day, I will never forget. There was a three-foot-tall upside-down cross with what looked to be a partial Jesus nailed to it with two dark colored wings coming out of both sides. It just sat there in the front window of the property and overlooked the neighborhood. I thought to myself, *No wonder they hate this place and think that it's evil.*

I pointed at the statue and asked what it was and why it was there. George said he'd never seen it before. I honestly didn't believe him. I think he knew it was there and tried to act as if he didn't so he wouldn't have to explain it. I looked at Greg and Stephanie and they both gave me a look that read *We'll talk about it later.* I held my tongue and didn't say any more to avoid upsetting George and getting ourselves kicked out of there.

I turned to look behind us and saw a spiral staircase leading to what looked to be a loft with several doors leading to different rooms. I made my way up the steps and everyone started to follow. As we got to the top of the stairs, I asked, "What are these rooms?" as I entered the first room I came to. George said this area was Mr. Wills's personal apartment. I looked to my right and saw a kitchen fully furnished from the late 1960s with appliances, cabinets, and sink still intact but not operational. It was a large empty room with stairs that stepped up into it. I turned to leave the room and heard a man's voice say something like "Who are you?" I turned and looked at everyone. They all at the same time asked who was that. Someone asked if someone was in the building, and George quickly sprinted out of the room and down the stairs to check if someone was there. He returned several moments later with a look of dismay on his face. He said he ran all the way downstairs and had seen no one.

I know what I heard had came from that room, and it sounded as if it was behind me, but to keep the sweep going, I dismissed it as noise coming from outside. I encouraged everyone to keep moving so we could actually get to investigating at some point. I quickly glanced into the other two rooms in the loft and saw that one had a hot tub that dated back to what looked to be the 1980s, and the other was a full-size barroom with a full bar that seated up to fifteen people. I was shocked that all this was still here and tucked away in this industrial-type apartment area in the building. Mr. Wills had worked his entire life and was an amazing business man who became very wealthy from his hard work and dedication to his community. He spared no expense when it came to his living situation in the building and spent a lot of time in that area of the property when he was not working.

As we moved back into the hallway, we only had one more area to cover: the train room, which is located in the attic (see page 173). George led the way down the hallway, past the caskets that littered the floor, to a door on the right side of the hall that was already open. We started walking up a long staircase and the heat was getting overbearing from the attic's poor ventilation and the fact attics are just hot.

The reason it is called the train room instead of the attic is it's basically a miniature train town setting that takes up three-quarters of the attic. When we got there, the miniature town looked more like a burned-out zombie apocalypse town with no signs of life or any toy trains. Only thing up there were more animal remains and piles of books, magazines, and newspapers dating back to the 1960s and the Civil Rights movement. There were actual pictures of Dr. Martin Luther King Jr. standing inside of the House of Wills in the early 1960s. It was amazing to have that history right there under our feet. It was just incredible to say the least. Rumor has it that Dr. King made a speech on the very stage in the large cathedral-like room.

I said to everyone that it looked like the place was clear and suggested we get out of there and get some air. Everyone was more than happy to exit the building at that point. We had searched the place for an hour and the heat and musty smells were getting to all of us. As we walked down the multiple flights of stairs to the exit, I couldn't help but feel on edge. By looking at everyone's faces, I knew it was going to be a long night. I don't think any of us were prepared for what lay ahead. Finally, we exited to fresh air and the sounds of the apartment building directly across the street. At that point, I didn't care that we were standing out in the open in one of the most dangerous areas in Cleveland, where drive-by shootings happen on a regular basis. As a matter of fact, right on the front steps of the House of Wills just a year or so before we were there, a man was gunned down and murdered in broad daylight. East Cleveland can be a very dangerous place and you must know the rules of the streets when visiting there or things can get really bad really quick for you. My best word of advice for visiting there is to keep your head down and mind your business.

I asked George if he wanted to stay and investigate for a while. He politely declined and said he had an early day tomorrow and maybe next time he'd join us. He said he was going to get ready to head out and for us to stay safe. As he started to walk back to his truck, I followed him and told him I had a question. I pulled him to the side and out of earshot of the others and asked if we had anything to really worry about from the neighborhood while we were there. He paused for a moment and made eye contact with me the whole time and said, "Yeah, it's possible." I then asked what he meant by that and if there would be a problem with us being there. He said some of the people around this area are pretty superstitious and believe the House of Wills is a curse on the whole neighborhood and it should be burned to the ground along with everything in it. He said many neighbors believe every bad thing that happens in a ten-block radius is because of this building. There were a few people around here that would like no more than to cause havoc and start problems. One in particular was a neighborhood leader of some sort, and the word on the street was that he was planning something. George continued, explaining that some neighbors were using any excuse to start a war because of the House of Wills and what they believed was happening in it.

I asked what he meant by "what is happening." He told me, "Ask Patty when she gets here. You saw with your own two eyes how the locals act. They won't even walk past the place without crossing the street first to avoid it." He explained they believed anyone who associated or went into the House of Wills were evil, including him. That's why he didn't stick around after dark anymore.

"This place has changed since Eric Freeman took it over and the neighborhood feels it," said George. "They have to live right across from it every day of their lives. We get to come and go as we please," he continued. "We will be here tonight stirring up the place and leave in the morning and leave the neighborhood to deal with it."

I asked George if he believed in the superstitions that the neighbors did. He declined to give his answer, but said, "That's what they believe and no one is going to be able to tell them any different at this point. We are the enemy to those people, and they don't want any of us here." George told me that when he said he had to go because he had an early day tomorrow, it was a lie. He didn't want to look scared in front of us, but he wouldn't stick around after dark.

"It's bad enough in broad daylight, but it gets really bad outside and inside that building after the sun goes down. You choose what one you want to deal with: the living out here or the dead in there," said George. In his book, both were equally as dangerous.

I asked George again why he didn't want to talk about what was going on at the House of Wills. He told me that he had no problems with anyone. He would mind his business and keep his head down. For George, this was a part time job, but he did it because he used to love being at the House of Wills, taking care of the location, and helping out when needed. Plus, he really didn't want to leave Patty here to do it on her own. He cared about her and didn't want to let her down, let alone leave her here to take care of all of this by herself. She was too attached to the building and wouldn't leave.

George wished me luck and safety, then walked back to his truck, got in, and drove off stone-faced without a wave goodbye. I could tell I hit a nerve with him and may have even pushed too far, but I was concerned about what he meant about certain things that were going on in the building. As I walked back to the others, they asked what that was all about. At the time, I did not want to say too much to them. I wasn't sure how much Stephanie and Greg knew about the place or if they were hiding anything from us at the time. They had been here several times before and I thought it was strange they did not show the same fear that George did. I kept my response short by saying George just gave me a heads up about the area, to keep our car doors locked, and that Patty would be by later.

I quickly changed the subject and suggested we start setting up equipment. Everyone agreed and started unpacking hard cases from the trunks of the cars and took them up to our base camp. As soon as I saw an opportunity, I grabbed Keith and explained to him exactly what George had told me outside. Keith, being as reserved as he could, said should we tell Stephanie and Greg? I almost hesitated to say no, but I then told him we should wait it out until Patty gets here, get her side of the story before jumping to conclusions, and that we should keep this to ourselves for the time being. I wanted to see how much they actually knew about this place and if we were being set up or if they were just as thrown off by all of it as we were. I didn't trust anyone besides the two of us until we got the whole story. Quite honestly, we really didn't know them that well. We only investigated with them one time in Gettysburg and that's it. We were hours from home and several states away. We didn't know anyone out there and needed to watch our backs. For all we knew, this could have been some kind of sick setup to lure us out there. Keith completely agreed with everything I said and was as concerned as I was. The way George talked, something was off there and we were in the middle of it, like it or not. I told Keith that if he saw anything strange at all or if something didn't feel right to let me know. I had a bad feeling about all of this and did not want to become some kind of statistic.

At this point, I wanted to get set up and start investigating the building. But at the same time, I had in the back of my head to keep an eye on everyone and watch out for any strange behavior. This is no way to go about a paranormal investigation, let alone be in a place like this one. I already felt off mentally and physically at this point, so any extra stress was not needed. It comforted me to know I had Keith with me to watch my back, and I knew he could handle his own if needed. The night was finally upon us at this point, and it was time to dig in and get this investigation going to see where the night would take us.

Chapter 6

The Beast

Two hours later, after we set up our equipment and made sure everything worked correctly, we were ready to finally investigate. That's right: ghost hunting, at its best, consists of hours of setup and breakdown. Hell, by the time you get set up, you're ready for bed. That was in my early days. Anyone who has investigated with me in the last several years knows I travel light these days; I can carry everything I need in a backpack.

We had several rem-pods set up in the first-floor hallway right where we first entered the building. We decided to set up base camp in the first room to the right at the top of the stairs for easy access to the cars to get equipment in and out at the end of the night. Honestly, looking back on it, I think we did it for an easy escape route if the s*** hit the fan.

JUST AS THE CREW WAS SETTING UP EQUIPMENT,
SOME OF THE EQUIPMENT ALERTED US TO AN ENTITY IN THE HALLWAY

As we loaded ourselves up with recorders and some other gadgets, one of the rem-pods at the far end of the hall started going off. On any given day, that wouldn't bother me in the least. It could be a battery dying or a walkie-talkie or a phone setting it off. But this was different. It would start and stop. It finally caught my attention when it happened multiple times. I walked to the door to look down the hall: nothing. I said, "If anyone is there, step forward.

Those lights won't hurt you." Just like clockwork, bang! The rem-pod went off. I immediately turned around to see where everyone was standing in the room and where their hands were to make sure they weren't goofing around. Everyone was on the up-and-up and no one was playing any kind of tomfoolery. I went back to try to communicate with whatever was setting the equipment off. I asked if the entity could step forward and set off the next rem-pod, and on demand, it did.

At this point, it was around ten at night and the place was darker than dark. The only light we had was from our flashlights and our camera monitors. I took it one step further and asked for the entity to come to the third rem-pod. Several seconds passed and, boom, it went off. At this point, I was getting a little excited and so was everyone else as they stood behind me in the doorway. I positioned myself in the hallway, crouched down so I could get a clear shot of the hall, then said, "I'm going to stand up and approach you." As soon as I went to stand, a dark shadow mass stepped away from the wall about five feet in front of me, paused for a few seconds, and then took off down the center of the hall. All the rem-pods went off one at a time in the order of the direction it was traveling.

I jumped back into the doorway, plowing through everyone, and yelled, "Please! Tell me you guys saw that!" Greg, Stephanie, and Keith all saw exactly what I saw and explained the encounter the exact same way I did. Getting activity this early in an investigation means you know you're in for one hell of a night. I believed that whatever, or whoever, that was, it was basically a scout for whatever alpha entity resided in the building. It was checking us out to see our strengths and weaknesses, figure out who was who, who was the alpha of our group, and if we would be able to cause any great harm to it.

Over the years, I have explored places like this that sit empty for long periods of time and have multiple spirits enter the location and make it their home. Spirits are drawn to it like a safe haven and they establish a community. Like any organization or community, there's usually a leader or an alpha that calls the shots. Light attracts light, dark attracts dark, so when you have a location like this that has had so many negative things happen in it over the years, it's going to attract things that are on the darker side. My theory is if a location has been used for negative things, it's going to attract the negative.

This was an exciting start to our investigation. We'd just had a really interesting encounter with something we all were able to see with our own eyes and had multiple devices go off. That was what we call "pay dirt" in the paranormal community. Now it was time to really dig in and start investigating.

Before we started exploring, we made up some simple rules. The first rule, given the sketchy history of the location, was that no one was to go anywhere alone, for safety reasons. That's a no-brainer, of course. The second rule was that if anyone started to feel off or not right, we needed to get them out of the building as fast as possible, given the history of people starting to act insane or crazy at this location. Greg and Stephanie knew of some other paranormal investigation groups that experienced these kinds of attacks on one or more occasion at the House of Wills and we wanted to keep everyone safe. Prior to the investigation at the House of Wills, I had never been on an investigation where people have actually lost their minds and tried to attack other group members. I had seen and heard a lot of things in my days of investigating, such as mediums saying they are being possessed or investigators saying they feel an evil presence, but nothing ever got physical. The night was still young, so I figured we'd see what would happen.

We crept, ever so carefully, down the same hallway we just saw the shadow anomaly dart down moments before. Every door we passed felt like a dark portal to another world. We hesitantly walked into what once was a waiting room at the end of the hallway. We stopped and stood quietly to listen for anything and stared at the dust-covered furniture sitting in the room as if it was frozen in time. Then, in the silence, we heard what sounded like footsteps. It sounded like they were coming from the staircase just outside the room that leads to the basement. I curiously leaned out the door to get a better gauge of where the footsteps were coming from. They were definitely headed downstairs. I looked over my shoulder at the group and gave a hand motion that pointed down. We quickly gathered our thoughts and emotions and started down the stairs, not knowing what was ahead of us. Was it our shadow friend from earlier, a trespasser, or something else we hadn't encountered yet? Slowly and methodically, we took our time on the steps to try and sneak up on whatever just entered the basement area. Thinking back to our experience, I look back on this moment and laugh. What were we thinking? Did we think we were actually going to capture a spirit and take it out of there with us or confront a trespasser and possibly end up shooting someone in self-defense? That would have gone over really well. I can see the news now: *Ghost hunters think they're shooting a ghost and end up shooting a local vagrant.* That would not be a good look at all.

We approached the bottom of the stairs and peered into the large room where we were earlier, which reminded me of a viewing area for funerals. We saw nothing as our flashlights shone through the room, hoping for a glimpse of something. We entered the room and hesitantly waited for the jump scare to come, but it was eerily quiet. Nothing; there wasn't even the sound of crickets in the summer's eve. I decided to walk down the several steps to the right of the doorway, which looked like it belonged in a medieval castle. Everyone followed me so as to not be left alone in the big room. We peered into the large room with the caskets for a moment, then decided to enter just to make sure no one was hiding there.

After several moments of searching the room, we found nothing, as suspected. Greg wanted to do an EVP session and use what's called a ghost box SB7 or hack shack. It has many names in the paranormal field. A ghost box SB7 is basically an AM/FM radio that is designed to scan through radio channels at a high rate of speed in the hopes of picking up a spirit's voice through white noise. This is all theory and not

DISEMBODIED FOOTSTEPS COULD BE HEARD GOING DOWN THIS STAIRWELL

scientifically proven in any way, but I've heard some pretty compelling responses over the years that make you scratch your head. With that said, Greg went into his EVP session. At the same time, Stephanie held a voice recorder while everyone took turns asking questions. This went on for several minutes until we started to hear what sounded like voices coming over the ghost box SB7.

For some reason, I told Greg to shut off the box because something didn't sound right. Greg shut the box off without hesitation. The box went silent, but the voices kept going. The voices we heard were not coming from the box but were audible in real time, out loud, in the room with us. Then, the voices suddenly stopped and we were all in shock. I believe every curse word in the English vocabulary was used by everyone in the room. As we stood there in shock, I tried to form a sentence to ask out loud and failed miserably. As I regained my composure, I asked, "Who are you?" Nothing, not a peep. I asked again, but louder this time. Once again, complete silence filled the room as we all looked over our shoulders and stared off into the darkness. Suddenly, I was hit with a feeling of sadness, sick to my stomach, and freezing cold. It was July and 85°F in that basement. I should not have felt cold. These feelings came on in seconds and out of nowhere.

I wondered if I ate something weird and why I was getting sick when I felt completely fine two minutes before that. Then, I noticed something as Keith's flashlight shined past me. I could see my breath. I quickly shined my light across the room at everyone else to see if I could see their breath. Nothing. I asked everyone to shine their lights on me to see if they could see my breath. Everyone said yes at the same time. They looked to see if they could see their own breath and then realized it was only happening to me. I started to feel even worse at this point and realized something was trying to attach itself to me. The only thing going through my head were the stories of investigators going crazy and getting violent. I told the group we needed to get out of the basement immediately and made a beeline for the steps. Everyone was on my coattails as we got out of there as fast as we could.

And then, just like that, everything went blank. I have no memory of what happened over the next couple of minutes. However, it was caught on video by Keith and the whole team was there to witnesses what happened. The video shows me stopping on the landing that leads to the first floor and staring off into the darkness. The video also captures the team trying to communicate with me. The video continues on, and after several moments, I walk up about six steps, stop, and yell, "Get off me now!" at the top of my lungs. Keith was on the landing directly behind me with the video camera pointing up while Greg and Stephanie were both at the top of the first-floor landing, looking down at me. As I yelled, a dark ball anomaly shot out of my right side and entered the wall to my right.

I woke up from this trancelike state while on the top landing, and Keith told me what he just captured on his video camera. At this point, I was very angry and did not want to talk about it. I walked back to base camp, grabbed a bottle of water, and downed it in almost one gulp. I started to gain my composure as they rallied around me to make sure I was okay. I could hear everyone talking to me and see what was going on around me, but I wasn't able to respond. I'd compare that feeling to being a puppet. It was as if I had no control over my limbs and was on autopilot. I tried to fight in my head to say something, and it took a lot of strength for me to yell when I did. I did not want to become another victim of this dark place. When I look back on the experience now, I'm glad I had the wherewithal to beat it, whatever the entity was, in the moment before it was able to get its hooks into me.

Chapter 7

The Enabler

I sat alone to catch my wits and looked at the wall in front of me, with its distressed Victorian wallpaper that hung on to the sickening decay underneath. Decay has a kind of beauty about it that can be explained only through taking it in and understanding what it once was before its fall. I was alone in my thoughts and tried to gather and understand what just happened to me. I briefly wondered if I had hallucinated what just happened. I remember thinking, *Am I even here right now? Is this a bad dream of some sort?* But I glanced up and saw the equipment in the room and heard Greg and Keith talking in the hallway. I then heard an unfamiliar voice, a female I didn't recognize. There were greetings from everyone in the hall as I sat and waited for this unfamiliar person to pass by the door so I could gather a glimpse of who it might be. A woman I did not recognize entered the room and took a seat in front of me, like she owned the place. I could tell she had been at the House of Wills many times before by the way she moved into the space, as if she could walk through the place blindfolded and never miss a step. She looked at me as I leaned against the wall and said, "You must be Daryl." It suddenly occurred to me, as I was pulled out of my dream state, that his had to be Patty, the other caretaker of the House of Wills.

I greeted her by extending my hand to shake hers. She took my hand, gripped it tightly, and said, "This place has already gotten into you, sir. I can tell by the look on your face."

I said, "You don't know the half of it."

She laughed, took a pause to look around the room, and asked how "they" were treating us so far. I smirked as Stephanie began to tell her about our events. I rudely cut her off and asked Patty what the hell was going on here. Patty turned to me and said she wasn't at liberty to talk about it. We all were drawn back by that answer. I asked what she meant, and she said, "He's the owner and the boss. and I need to respect that. He's misunderstood."

I asked her to clarify, but, instead, she answered a question with a question, asking if George said anything to me. I quickly thought, *How do I answer this and get something out of her?* I bluntly said yes, he did, but that she would fill us in the rest of way. She rocked back and forth for several seconds. I could tell she was nervous and scared to say too much. Greg asked her to tell us about the statues in the cathedral we saw from the balcony since Keith and I hadn't seen them up close yet. Patty then began to talk.

She started the conversation by saying this place used to be such a beautiful, peaceful building. She used to spend the nights there by herself all the time. She would go upstairs and sleep in the coffin in the apartment area. I stopped her right there and asked her to clarify that statement. She laughed and said, "It sounds strange, but it was very peaceful."

She said, in the past, she tried to make contact with whomever was there. At the time, the spirits there were at peace and were happy. Patty had been a caretaker there long before Eric Freeman ever owned it. She was the caretaker when he bought the building, so he kind of adopted her and kept her on to help take care of the place when Eric was away. Patty explained that Eric knew how much she loved House of Wills, so they had a sort of agreement.

While Patty was explaining this, she kept referring to Eric in the third person, so I had to ask who she was referring to. I also asked what changed when he took over House of Wills and why it no longer was the peaceful place she remembered. After what I had just gone through and the negative energy felt in the building, I had a hard time believing it was ever a good and peaceful place as Patty described.

Patty said when Eric first took ownership of the House of Wills, not much changed. Everything seemed fine, as if it was a good transition of ownership. Everything went on as normal. Patty would come over after her day job to check on the place and make sure all was well. About a month or so in, however, she started to notice little changes. The mood of the building started to feel different, as if it was unsteady. She said the energy started to feel completely different over the next couple of months. It seemed as if the spirits were getting restless and upset about something. At first, she thought it was just her and shrugged it off, but it got worse. She noticed how, even during the day, the sunlight would not shine through the windows, as if something was blocking it out.

One night, at about two in the morning, she got a call from a paranormal group that was conducting an investigation. They needed her to come over quickly. Something was happening and they didn't know what to do; it was an emergency. Patty asked them if someone was injured, and they said no, they couldn't explain it. They just needed help. She rushed over in the middle of the night, not knowing what she would walk into.

Patty pulled up and saw all of their cars still parked out front and assumed all was good so she walked into the garage area and could hear screaming and yelling. She quickly ran upstairs and followed the screams until they led her into the cathedral, where she witnessed the lead investigator lying on the floor with three investigators holding him down as he cursed them and screamed that he was going to kill everyone in the room. Patty quickly ran over and tried talking to him to calm him down, but it did not work. She told the other investigators they needed to get him out of the building by any means possible. They all dragged him, kicking and screaming, through the building and were able to get him out the side door. As soon as he was out of the building, he was fine and didn't remember anything that happened.

He could not even remember starting the investigation hours before. Patty said he then broke down and started crying. He was obviously very traumatized by what just happened. Patty asked the rest of the team if this behavior was normal for him and every one of them said they had never seen anything like this on an investigation before. They were all very shaken, so they packed up their gear as he sat in the car and then left. They never asked to do another investigation at the building.

At the time, I did not know what to think because I was still shaken by what happened to me. I filed the information away and wondered if that event had to do with the sudden change in energy in the building that Patty had described. I asked Patty if she thought it was strange that this guy went crazy like that for no reason and was fine as soon as he was taken out of the building by force. She said she didn't think it strange at the time, but that changed after what happened to her several weeks later. I asked her what happened, but I almost didn't want to know. But I allowed her to continue with her next explanation on how messed up the House of Wills was.

She said she was attacked, and I asked if she meant the man with the axe that George told us about. Patty began to explain that she stopped to check on the building one day after work, as always. She pulled into the side parking lot, and at the time the place looked calm and peaceful. She entered the building through the side door like always and started making the rounds. When she got to the top of the first floor, something felt off and wasn't right. She turned on her flashlight and made her way down the hallway to the staircase on the other side that leads to the other floors. She kept looking behind her like someone was in the building, but she didn't hear anything; it was a feeling or sixth sense of sorts.

Patty started to hurry through her check and go. She had never felt like this in the building before. She started to walk up the staircase to the second floor and that's when all her fears came true. Standing at the top of the stairs on the third-floor landing was a man holding an axe. He made direct eye contact with Patty and charged down the stairs toward her. She immediately turned and ran. He didn't say anything as he chased her through the building. Patty felt at any moment she was going to feel the sharp blade of the axe pierce her back. She kept running as fast as she could. If she could make it outside, she knew she had a fighting chance because she had a gun in the car.

Patty made it down the hallway and didn't dare turn around because she could hear and feel his disgusting breath only feet away. She quickly ran down the stairs leading to the garage and completely skipped over the hole in the stairs as if it wasn't even there. She rammed the door open with her shoulder so hard she almost dislocated it. Finally, she was just a few steps from her car. She raised her car keys to unlock the doors, grabbed the car door and swung it open with such force that it bounced back and hit her in the back as she reached for her purse to grab the gun in it. The force of the door knocked her face-first into the car. The pain from it was so insanely sharp that she actually thought he had hit her with the axe. She wrapped her hand around the grip of the gun and quickly swung around to point the gun at anything that moved. With her heart racing, she looked around and saw no one. She turned to the side door of the building and he was nowhere in sight. Patty quickly scanned her surroundings but no one was there. She jumped into the car, locked it, and dialed 911. She fixed eyes on the side door to be sure no one left the building until the police arrived. Three patrol cars and an unmarked unit pulled into the parking lot. With guns drawn, two officers approached her car, and she explained what happened. Five officers entered the building while two of the uniformed officers stayed with Patty. Almost twenty minutes went by. One of the officers outside kept radio contact with the ones inside as they cleared each floor. They found nothing. There was not a trace of the man. The axe was neatly placed on the stage in the cathedral, almost as an offering of sorts.

After that, Patty needed to ask Eric some questions to figure out why the energy had changed so much after he purchased it. On a day she knew he was moving his artwork into the building, Patty made a visit to speak to Eric.

Patty pulled up to the side entrance and saw a large truck parked next to the front doors, which were open. She had been a caretaker there for many years and had never seen those doors open. They had always been nailed shut and locked. Patty parked next to the truck and came in through the open doors, since in all the years she'd been there she never had the opportunity. The place was quiet, then she heard what sounded like a full-on conversation being held in the cathedral. She figured it must have been

Eric and the movers or whomever came to help him. She walked into the cathedral and stood in disbelief as she saw four large wooden hand-carved statues standing in the middle of the room. Two of them stood at least eight foot tall and the other two were around seven feet. Eric was in the room by himself, and when asked about the statues, he said he carved them himself. Patty described them as something out of someone's nightmare.

Patty steeled up her courage and asked what he had brought there. The atmosphere had changed since he took over, and she wanted to know what was happening. He told her that he belonged to the Church of Satan and that it was nothing like what is portrayed in TV or in movies. He said the group was peaceful, stayed to themselves, and hid from the outside world in their own church. They worship Beelzebub the rebel angel, who was cast from Heaven for not obeying God's laws. They are the true believers of the angel of music, and their beliefs differ from what has been written about them. Most of what they do originates from Christianity and has been villainized over the decades by outside influences. It's neither good nor evil.

After Eric walked away, Patty started to walk out of the building when something from the top balcony caught her eye. She looked up and saw a man dressed in an all-white suit sitting there and watching her. She waved at him and received no response. She then realized she couldn't see any facial features, almost as if he didn't have a face at all. She walked toward the staircase that leads to the second floor and he stood up and started walking to the double doors on the same floor. She moved up the steps as fast as she could, and when she reached the second-floor hall, she should have met him in the hallway, but there was no sign of the man in white. It had only been fifteen or twenty seconds between the time she saw him and when he disappeared. She searched the second and third floors and saw no one.

When Patty headed up the steps to the apartment area, she was met by Eric at the top of the stairs. She asked Eric who was the man in the white suit? He looked at her as if he had no idea what she was talking about and repeated that he was the only one in the building. Patty explained what she saw to him and he seemed as confused as her. He said he'd check the building, but that he'd see Patty out of the building safely. As Patty pulled away from the building that day, she felt like her whole world had caved in. The building she loved for so many years had dramatically changed and there was nothing she could do to stop it.

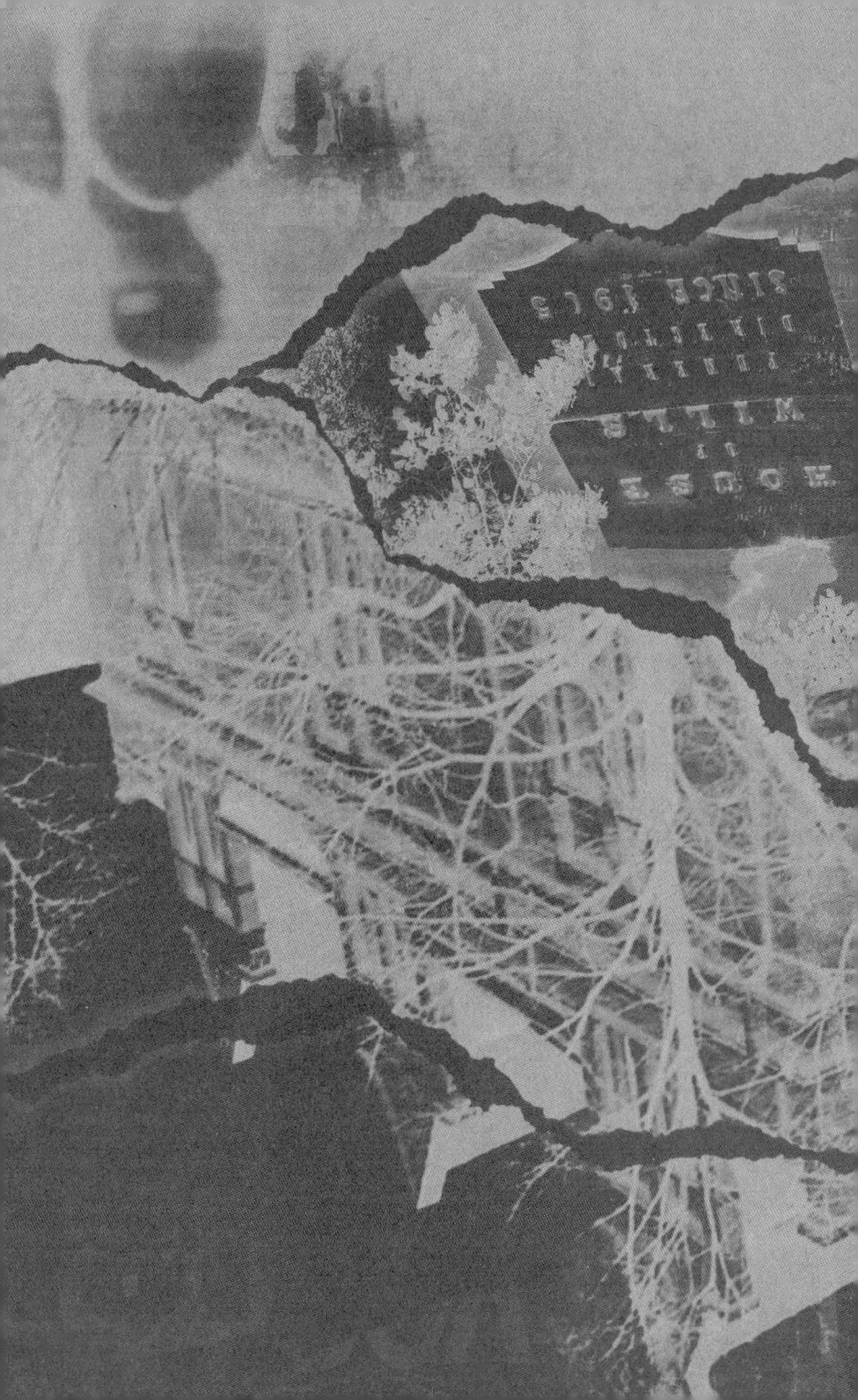

Chapter 8

The Entity

We all sat quietly in the room digesting the story Patty just told about our gracious host Eric. Now what? Do we leave now and hope to keep our sanity intact or do we carry on with the investigation? I was honestly upset that I did not know these things before I came all the way here to put Keith and myself in danger. I stood up, thanked Patty for her honesty, and said that I was going outside to get some air. Keith followed me outside and we sat in the car for several moments and were speechless, not knowing our next move. Patty, Stephanie, and Greg soon joined us beside our car. I had the keys in the ignition and wanted to turn them, throw the car in reverse, and hightail it back home, but something stopped me. We exited the car to have a conversation with the others. Keith was deadly silent. I could tell he was deeply bothered by what he heard, as was I. Patty said a couple words to start some small talk to ease the tension, but I honestly didn't hear a word she said. She bid us farewell, got in her car, and left as abruptly as she came, like a thief in the night, and left us to deal with the situation at hand.

I asked Stephanie and Greg if they knew about any of that before they dragged us here. Stephanie said no, as if she was insulted, and asked why I would ask such a thing. Greg spoke up and said the only thing he knew about was Patty being attacked with an axe. The reality was that we had two choices, leave or stay, and I did not drive all this way for nothing. I asked Keith how he was feeling, There was a pause then he answered: "Let's do this." Greg said he was still in, Stephanie too. However, Stephanie said we needed to do a prayer before we continued on and she had something she wanted us to have just in case. I was not much of a prayer guy at the time and actually rolled my eyes when she said it, but if it was going to make anyone feel better, I was all for it. Stephanie popped the trunk of her car and frantically tore through a bag as she looked for something. She then handed Keith and me sage. I sarcastically asked what she wanted me to do with it, and she said we needed to light it and wave the smoke around ourselves before leaving in the morning.

Everyone gathered in a circle and held hands as Stephanie lead the prayer. I don't remember a word she said, and it wasn't because I didn't care. I started going into a dreamlike state again, much like before but not as bad. I envisioned myself laughing during the prayer and, when the prayer was done, trying to hurt all three of them in a way I wouldn't dare mention. The next thing I remember, the prayer was over and we went back inside. I grabbed Keith and pulled him to the side as Stephanie and Greg entered the building.

"Man, something is wrong," I said.

Keith, shockingly, said, "You too?"

I asked what he meant, and he described having the same exact vision I just had during the prayer, except he was the one doing terrible things. I was blown away by what he said. I told him we all needed to keep our eye on each other and if anyone started acting differently, we pull everyone from the building immediately, no questions asked. Something was trying to play us all against each other and it wasn't good.

Keith and I entered the building with hesitation, and we soon caught up with Stephanie and Greg. I wanted to see the statues, so I suggested we restart our investigation in the cathedral (see page 175). We gathered our gear and headed to the stage area. We entered the cathedral stage right, at the exact same spot Patty spotted the man in white. I couldn't help but wonder what she saw. Maybe someone who died in this building was not happy with the way things were changing. When I thought back to Patty's story, it all seemed plausible to me. I don't think Eric had anything to do with it as far as a prank because he didn't even know Patty was stopping by that day.

It was dark but I could see the outline of some large objects in the middle of the room in front of the pews. I shined my light toward them, and they were exactly as Patty described. They all resembled medieval torture devices, with a hint of S&M and satanic belief rolled into one. They were almost indescribable, and it was hard to believe they were all hand-carved. It must have taken years to make them all. This was Keith's and my first time seeing these statues and we didn't know what to say. Stephanie and Greg had already seen them before but were still in awe of them.

It was already after midnight, so we started setting up some handheld cameras. Greg said he had an experiment he wanted to try out. He said since this was a place of worship and a funeral home, we should play some gospel music on some Bluetooth speakers and get the ghost box going at the same time. I said, "All right, let's go, but if anyone starts feeling off in any way, we need to let the others know."

Everyone agreed to keep an eye on one another and themselves. Greg turned on the music as loud as his tiny speakers would allow. The ghost box started to sweep through the channels at a high rate of speed and pierced the air. We sat and listened as each played over the other. It went on for several minutes until I finally had enough of the ghost box and told him to turn it off. Greg laughed and agreed that it was a little much with both of them going at the same time.

We left the music playing, and then we heard a loud crash come from the back of the room. We all jumped back and shined our lights toward the direction the sound came from, but there was nothing there. Greg started to approach the large double doors, and as I started to follow him, we heard a loud bang on the doors in front of him, Greg jumped back in fear, and I stopped in my tracks and waited for someone to break through the doors, but nothing happened. We quickly opened both doors, only to see darkness and no one standing there. I turned to Stephanie and Keith, who were still standing in the middle of the room, and asked if they heard that. They both replied yes. They could hear it all the way over where they were standing, even with the music playing. Greg and I decided to leave the doors open as we walked away to see what else would happen.

We went back to the center of the room and stood there just listening and waiting. Several moments passed and nothing happened, but I noticed everyone looked drained of energy. Then the music started to sound like it was slowing down and the room felt as if it was moving around us. I asked the others if they felt and heard this and they all said yes. It was as if we were standing in the middle of a ballroom and people were spinning and dancing around us as we stood still. It was as if we were getting a glance back in time at a social gathering that may have taken place at the House of Wills. We couldn't see the entities, but we could feel the air moving around us, and it was almost as if we could slightly hear laughter and joy coming from outside our circle of the four of us. I wanted to tell Greg to turn off the music, but in a strange way I was enjoying it, as we all were. It felt magical and delightful. After several moments of this, I noticed Stephanie slump to the floor, as if she was starting to fall asleep. Keith did the same thing. I quickly saw what was happening and reached to turn off the music. As I did, Greg grabbed it from me, as if to say, "Don't touch it." I quickly grabbed it from his hands, turned it off, and threw it to the floor. Immediately, it all stopped. Dead silence filled the room.

Everyone's behavior started to return to normal. It was as if we were under a trance or stuck in a moment in time. Greg looked at his watch, then pulled out his phone to check the time and asked us what we had. Keith said his phone read two in the morning. Greg said that it didn't seem possible, but his read the same thing. I looked at my phone and it read the same: two in the morning. Stephanie blurted out that it couldn't be right. We had only been in there for about thirty minutes, at the most, and when we came into the room, it was a little after midnight. Over two hours passed but it felt as if time stood still for us in the moment. The real world kept going without us even noticing. None of us knew what to make of it, but we knew we had lost almost two hours and could only remember about twenty minutes of it.

We decided to go back and look at our handheld cameras and see what happened. When we reviewed the footage, it was literally two hours of us standing in a circle with gospel music playing in the background. But then we noticed something that still, to this day, sends a chill up my spine. There's a point before we start the ghost box and music experiment where I am standing next to a statue and something decided to make itself known. At some point, Keith put the camera he was holding on one of the pews that pointed in the direction I was standing. What it captured was mind-blowing. The video showed me talking to the rest of the group, who are just out of view of the camera. Out of nowhere, a dark mass grows up from the floor and stands directly behind me and just left of the statue. The only way I can explain what it looked like is to imagine what the angel of death would look like. It was tall and dark with what looked to be a hooded cloak over its entire body. It just stood there and watched me for several moments until it melted back into the floor.

At this point, after seeing that and experiencing the loss of time, I decided we needed to take a break and wrap our heads around what just happened. We quickly started grabbing what we could so we could get out of that area. We started moving toward the stage doors to exit when a sound, which I will never forget, cut straight through the air and stopped all of us dead in our tracks. We quickly turned to see what creature was just released from hell, but we saw nothing. We could only hear the sounds of what one would imagine to be a demon screaming in complete hatred of everything good in the world. The screaming came from the balcony. It started on the left side of the room and followed the entire balcony, all the way around to the right, above where we were standing. Then, it was dead silence. We stood in complete disbelief at what we just heard. It was like whatever in that room was disgusted with us because it couldn't get its hooks into our souls. At about the same time, we all yelled, "What in the f*** was that?!" I told everyone to leave the room, now. They quickly made for the door as I backed out of the room. I didn't dare turn my back on whatever that was.

I made it to the door, where they all waited for me, and we headed for the exit to get out of the building. We finally made it outside and headed to the side parking lot. In what I can only describe as a moment of relief for all of us, we started laughing. We critiqued each other's reactions in the moment, but it was just our way of relieving the tension. Then reality kicked in. We hadto go back in the building because all of our equipment is still in there. By this time, it was almost three in the morning and we still ha about two and a half hours before dawn. I give everyone an option. We can go in and pack up now and roll out, or we can stick it out until dawn. I was all for staying so we could say we made it until first light since we were told no one made it though an entire night and most people leave before sunrise. I know I might get some flack for that last statement from some of the groups that have been there before, but I'm only going on what I have been told. Maybe some of them left because they were done with their investigations. I honestly don't know. But I do know one thing, and that is I'm not going to be part of the statistics of this location. If we can be the first, then be it. The looks on their faces said they were ready to pack it in. I told them I did not drive all this way to get my ass kicked by this place and I'm going back in, and they can do what they want.

I started walking toward the door to go back in, and in the back of my mind, I was saying, *Please someone stop me*. I heard footsteps behind me and turned to see Keith behind me. He didn't say a word but quietly followed my every step. I then saw Stephanie and Greg join us as we walked back to base camp.

We all gathered in front of the monitors that showed the lockdown cameras placed throughout the building. I pointed to the one screen of a room I didn't recognize. Greg said it was the Egyptian room, which got its name because it's decorated like a pharaoh's tomb and painted in gold trim. He then explained all the strange things that happened to them the last time he was there and that he refused to go back in there. Stephanie said she would not go past the doorway. I wanted to check it out, so I told them to hang out in the hallway while I checked it out.

GREG SAID THAT DURING A PREVIOUS VISIT HE EXPERIENCED A NUMBER OF STRANGE THINGS IN THE ROOM DUBBED THE "EGYPTIAN ROOM," SO NAMED GIVEN ITS EGYPTIAN-LIKE DÉCOR

We headed down the long hallway where we all witnessed the shadow figure running from us earlier in the night. We went down a flight of steps into what looked like a waiting area decorated in gold trim and dark red colors. We were standing outside the cathedral but on the opposite side from where we had been earlier. I pointed and mentioned that the doors ahead of us was where we heard the loud bang from earlier. I could tell Greg and Stephanie were very uneasy in this area of the building. There were mirrors that lined the walls on both sides, and Greg said out loud with disdain in his voice, "I hate mirrors!" I asked Greg why he didn't like mirrors and he explained he had a bad experience in that exact room with the mirrors. He then took a long pause, as if he was hesitant or afraid to say what happened.

Stephanie asked Greg if it was okay for her to say what happened in there, and Greg said, in an almost disgruntled voice, to go for it. Stephanie told us about their investigation in the House of Wills the year before. It had been a relatively quiet investigation, but it was when they reached this room with the mirrors that everything went wrong. They tried an experiment they had heard about from some other investigators. They said if you place two mirrors facing each other and stand in between them and stare into one, things will happen. I asked what kind of things will happen, and Greg said, "Bad things obviously, as you can tell by the way I don't use mirrors anymore." I then did something unintentionally that I immediately regretted. I sarcastically laughed at what Greg just said. I was met with a disdainful look from Greg, and I followed it up with, "You mean to tell me you never use a mirror at home to see how you look before you leave the house or anything?" He said no angrily and walked away.

Stephanie explained that they set the experiment up by using the mirrors in the room and they had never tried it before until that night. They had no idea if it would work or not. She went first and stood in between the two mirrors and stared into the one she was facing. She said it felt like it was forever, but in reality, it was less than ten minutes. She said the only thing she really felt was light-headed for a moment and that the room felt as if it got colder, especially around her, but that was it. She said Greg laughed about how he thought the experiment was a joke and it was a waste of time. At first, he didn't want to partake in it, but she coaxed him into it, for which she felt so guilty for doing.

DURING A PREVIOUS INVESTIGATION, GREG HAD A FRIGHTENING EXPERIENCE
WHILE FACING THE MIRROR IN THIS ROOM

Greg stepped between the two mirrors and it started out as uneventful. He made joking remarks every minute or so. Then, the room grew colder and Greg was quieter with each passing moment, as if he was slipping further away each second. Stephanie started asking Greg questions about what he was feeling but he wasn't responding. At first, she thought he was joking around and messing with her, but she noticed a strange grin on his face while he was staring into the mirror. This went on for several minutes and it scared her to the point that she started yelling at him to stop. She was almost to the point of leaving because she felt unsafe, but she couldn't leave Greg there by himself, and she definitely did not want to travel through the building alone to leave. All of a sudden, Greg had a look of fear on his face as if he was being forced to see something that frightened him and was not able to look away or even blink to not see whatever it was he was experiencing. She said he looked as if he was in pain and was breathing heavily. She panicked, grabbed his arm, and yanked him out of the mirrors. He immediately collapsed and it looked as if he was going to start crying but was holding it back. He kept looking as if he was waiting for someone or something to come out of the mirrors. She asked what he saw, but he wouldn't answer. He kept looking back to see if it followed him. She feared for both of them at that point and didn't know what to do next: stay or run.

I asked Stephanie if he ever told her what he saw that night. She said he did, but not in any way she could understand at the time. He rambled on about seeing himself but a different version of himself: an evil version of sorts, like a doppelgänger. After he told her this, she packed up their equipment, left the building, and headed home.

It was a forty-minute drive back home and Stephanie wanted to make sure Greg was okay before she dropped him off at home to his fiancée and kids. She asked him again to explain slowly what happened in there. At this point, he seemed like he had calmed down for the most part and was more coherent and speaking normally. She asked him to start from the beginning and tell her everything the way he saw it. He said at first he saw nothing but his reflection in the mirror and thought it was a joke. But then he said his reflection started smiling at him, so without thinking about it he started smiling back. He said the background in the mirror was brighter than the room they were in and he could see almost everything in the room as if it was lit up like the middle of the day. He said the smile slowly turned into a horrible menacing grin with elongated teeth, and the eyes changed and grew wider and darker, as dark as the night sky. He felt frozen and couldn't move or blink; it felt like hours had passed, and this thing wasn't going to let him leave. It just stared back at him and mimicked his every move and expression. All he remembered after that was Stephanie pulling him away and the fear that it was not done with him yet.

After Stephanie dropped him off, she couldn't stop thinking about what she had done. Did she open up Pandora's box or was it all just a hallucination in Greg's head? She had never seen him like that before and hoped to never see him like that again. He is her closest friend and loves him like a brother. If what he saw was real, it was all her fault for forcing him to do the stupid experiment in the first place. Stephanie felt responsible for what happened that night. Whether it was real or not, it felt real to him.

The House of Wills plays with your head. Stephanie said Greg had been addicted to the House of Wills ever since that night. She said he would bring it up in almost every conversation, some way or somehow. He told her sometimes he would drive there in the middle of the night and just sit in the parking lot and stare at the building for hours until he was chased off by the locals or if his family called him.

"Why do you think he was so hell-bent on getting you guys here and he didn't mention any of this to you until you got here?" asked Stephanie.

She continued, "He's addicted to this horrible place and the only reason I'm here is because if I didn't come with him, he would find a way to come by himself. And I can't ever let that happen."

At that point, I didn't know what to think. Did Greg hallucinate the whole thing when he was staring into the mirror, or did he really see this altered personality of himself that night? There is a thing called pareidolia where in certain pictures or videos you may see an image of what looks to be a person or some other object that the viewer perceives to be a ghost or spirit. That could have been what Greg actually saw that night, but to me, the way it was explained, there was way too much detail and it was in real time. Not to mention that the interaction went on for several minutes in real time. As we talked, I looked in the direction where Greg was standing when he walked away and he was no longer standing there. I asked Keith where Greg went, and Keith shrugged his shoulders and said he didn't know. He was listening to Stephanie.

I made a beeline to the doorway closest to us and shined my flashlight down the long dark hallway. I saw nothing but a few empty highback antique chairs lining both sides of the hallway. The chairs looked as if they had been sitting in the same position since the building's heyday. I called out Greg's name but heard nothing, just silence. I called it again and

THE HALLWAY BETWEEN THE CATHEDRAL AND
THE EGYPTIAN AND ARCHIVE ROOM

still heard nothing. I started walking down the hallway and came to what looked to be another hallway but smaller (see page 175). When I looked up, I saw Greg standing there and staring into the dark. I asked him what the deal was and if he heard me calling his name. He replied no, and when I asked if he was okay, he said he was fine and just felt drawn to that area.

I asked if they had been in this area before or if it was new to them. Greg said they had been there before, and that the hall led to the artifacts room. He said the first time they visited, they felt uneasy when they tried going in the room. Stephanie said, in a stern voice, that we should stay out of there if we know what's good for us, as if to warn us.

At this point, I was fed up with the warnings and folk-lore. In a sarcastic tone I said, "You're not me and I am going in the room."

I was tired and had driven all this way and I was not here to just observe from a distance. I was going into that room regardless of what was on the other side of that threshold. I walked to the doorway and shined my flashlight into the pitch-black room. As I walked into the room, the first thing that got my attention was a large table in the middle of the room. In the middle of the table was a life-size statue of what looked to be a human split down the center from head to toe that showed its internal organs. I was immediately taken aback by the sight of it. I said, "What the hell is this?" I heard a voice from the hallway reply, "I told you so!"

DEBRIS-LITTERED, SOGGY, DECAYING CARPET

As I moved farther into the room, Keith broke off and headed into the adjacent room to our left. I headed deeper into the larger of the two rooms and cleared a path in the clutter of old broken relics and debris on the floor. I pulled out my phone to use as a camera and started snapping pictures in groups of three in the same direction. The reason I take them in threes is so when I go back and review them, I have a reference point on each of the pictures. If for some reason I do capture something in the shot that I don't see in real time, I can see if it's in all three pictures or just one. This way I know if I actually captured something or not.

As I walked through the room, I could feel the decaying, wet carpet underneath my feet, which probably dated back to the early 1970s, when the building had seen much better days. I made my way to a large hutch with broken glass doors that was filled with old newspaper clippings from the 1960s. I understood why Stephanie and Greg didn't want to enter this room. It had an ominous feeling about it, as if you were being watched by some unseen force. It felt as if you had trespassed into someone's private home. But it wasn't enough to stop me from searching through the piles of history and the macabre artifacts.

Suddenly, I heard Keith call me into the other room. I made my way through the debris until I found him standing in the back of the room, where he was shining his flashlight on another large statue that looked to be cut in half and nailed to a long wooden plank. I suggested to Keith that we head out of the room. I had had enough of the strange statues and relics and the rank musty smell of the wet carpet.

We headed back into the hallway, where Stephanie and Greg peered through the door and waited for our return. Greg asked what it felt like in there. I had to admit it felt a bit strange with all that was going on in there. With me being a complete skeptic, I thought maybe the feelings we all were getting in that room were due to the possibility of mold caused by the leaking roof. No sooner than I was thinking that, a loud disembodied voice came from the room that startled all of us and stopped us dead in our tracks. It was so loud and prominent I could swear it was a living person. But knowing there was only one way in and out of that room and we just left there, no one was in there but us. To this day, none of us are exactly sure what the voice said, but at the time it sounded like it said, "Believe!" I quickly shined my flashlight back into the room and we saw nothing. No movement, not a sound. I yelled, "Can you please say that again?!" Nothing but the sounds of our heavy breathing filled the room. I asked again for the voice to repeat. There was still nothing except dead silence. I suggested we do an EVP session while we were getting activity.

Stephanie brought out her recorder and we started in with the questions. We ended up doing multiple burst sessions where we use a voice recorder and let it record for a minute or two while we ask control questions. Then, we'd play it back to see if there was a response. We did that for twenty minutes and got nothing in return. I then suggested we move to another location in the building. Apparently, our friend had left us or had nothing else to say. Everyone agreed and Greg suggested we go to the attic, a.k.a. the train room (see page 173).

While we walked down the long hallway away from the artifacts room, I couldn't help but keep playing the voice from earlier over in my head. What did it mean by "believe"? Believe what? Was it because I dismissed the feelings we all were having? Was it reading my mind and my thoughts? If this thing was that intelligent, what else was it capable of doing? How strong was it really and was this the same thing Greg encountered last time he was here? I still had a lot of questions and hopefully I could get some answers before I left this insanely mysterious place called the House of Wills.

Chapter 9

The Wicket

We climbed the stairs heading to the train room as if we were walking to the gallows. I never saw four people take so long to climb three staircases. We walked down the hallway that led to the attic area called the "train room." Everyone, including myself, was beat, but we were not going to let a little fatigue and lack of sleep stop us. Keith and I were going on twenty-four hours straight of no sleep and still had an eight-hour ride ahead of us to make it home in time for work on Monday.

We finally made it to the train room and I remembered why we were avoiding it (see page 173). Besides the clutter and dead animal carcasses that littered the floor, it was the heat! It was at least twenty degrees hotter up in the attic compared to the first floor. It was hard to breathe, but we needed to try and make contact with someone, if possible. In all honesty, we could have called it quits with all we had been through, but for some reason I was dead set on going until sunrise. I don't know if it was pride or just pure stubbornness. Most investigators would have run out of the building after what we had experienced and never return. I decided we should just sit and do a burst EVP session. We did that for about twenty minutes and didn't get any responses.

I was getting ready to say let's head down to the apartment area when we all heard what sounded like someone trying to break into the building or possibly messing with our cars. We quickly ran down to a window on the second floor staircase where we could get a good view of the side parking lot. Nothing. The noise had stopped. Then a loud crash came from what sounded like the garage door we entered to get into the building. We all could plainly see the door from our vantage point and there was no one and nothing there. We decided to take a closer look and headed to the garage to see if anyone had broken into the building. When we got there, the door was still bolted shut the way we left it. Nothing looked to be disturbed or out of place. Suddenly a loud bang came from the outside of the garage door. It startled all of us. We stood quietly for a moment to wait and see if we heard anything else.

This next part gets a little tense, but it had to be done for everyone's safety and well-being. I told them we had to go out and check if anything was out there. I wasn't thinking paranormal at this point; I was thinking someone was on the other side of the door with weapons of their own. I carefully placed my hand on my sidearm and nodded to

Greg to unbolt the door and open it quickly. Keith was to my left and at the ready as well. The door flew open, and at first contact, I saw nothing. I told Keith, "I'm going right; you take the left of the cars that are parked outside of the door." I cautiously went right and cleared my corners as Keith went left and did the same. We met at the back of the vehicles and were clueless to what we heard. There was no one in sight, and the streets were quiet. We decided to walk to the street to see if we could see anyone. Nothing, not a soul to be seen for blocks. East Cleveland was surprisingly quiet at that moment. We started to walk back to the building where Greg and Stephanie were standing when we heard what sounded like a car driving past the building. We looked over our shoulders to see a patrol car slowly passing as the two officers paid us no attention. They turned their lights and sirens on and hit the gas to speed off to whatever call they just received. The moment was eerie and was a quick reminder of where we were. I told everyone I had no idea what that was. They agreed that it definitely sounded as if someone hit the door. I am in no way saying what happened was paranormal, but some of these places where we go to investigate can be in some real unsavory areas. It comes with the territory of paranormal investigations and should not be taken lightly.

I said, "Okay, let's finish this and get out of here."

Greg said, "All right, I'll start packing everything up if you grab the lockdown cameras."

"Hold up, that's not what I meant," I said. "Let's hit the apartment area and then we can get out of here."

Greg laughed and said that's what he meant, he was just kidding. Yeah, I'm not sure I believed that. I knew he wanted to get out of there. Believe me, we all did, but I was not leaving until the sun came up and I meant it.

We all started the trek back to the second floor, where the apartment loft is located (see page 174). When we approached the two large double doors that lead into the apartment, Stephanie stopped dead in her tracks in front of us all. Keith asked what was wrong. She asked, "Can you hear that?"

We stopped talking and listened closely. I couldn't hear anything and asked what she was hearing, but Greg shook his head as if to say, *Yeah, I hear it too.* My ears started to tune in to what sounded like a full-on conversation coming from the apartment. I moved to the front of everyone, opened the door, and the conversation, surprisingly, kept going. We entered the room slowly to not make too much noise. We all stood there dumbfounded because we could hear two or three people talking in low voices as if to keep it a secret meeting to themselves. Strangely enough, the voices sounded as if they moved to the loft area of the apartment. I started to head up the steps to the loft. I turned and looked at everyone else and they were not following. I shrugged at them, not saying a word, but trying to communicate *What are you guys waiting for? Let's go.*

I reached the top of loft and started to enter what was once Mr. Wills's private bedroom and the conversation abruptly came to an end. I said the first thing that came to mind, "Sorry, everyone. I should have knocked first." I turned and looked down at my three friends standing at the bottom of the steps, like deer caught in the headlights of an eighteen-wheeler. Keith asked if I saw anything. I said no, but the talking stopped when I entered the room.

The three of them met me at the top of the loft, and Greg suggested we try the spirit box. I started to roll my eyes but decided against it. I said, "Okay, let's do it, and maybe we will get something with it." Quite honestly, I was too tired to argue.

We all took separate corners of the room and sat on the floor. The floor was covered with a thin layer of dust, but we were all too tired to even care at that point. Greg fumbled with his spirit box and tried to see the settings until Stephanie shined her light in his direction to help him out.

The calm of the room was interrupted by the sound of AM and FM radio stations sweeping across each other at a high rate of speed. Personally, I never could stand the sound of these ghost boxes, never mind the fact that they leave too much room for false positives, in my opinion, but to each their own. Greg and Stephanie took turns asking questions. At some point, one of them asked what the name of location was. Several seconds passed, then we heard "House of Wills."

I immediately woke up from my coma-induced ghost box session and asked, "Did that say what I think it said?" "Yes," answered both Keith and Greg, repeating the phrase "House of Wills." We decided to slow down, take our time, and ask some control questions to see if we'd get some definitive answers.

I asked, "What city are we in?" Several seconds passed and then we heard "Cleveland, Ohio." It didn't give me just the city, but the state as well. I don't know why I was surprised by this after the night we'd had so far, but for some reason I felt like we were talking to Mr. Wills. I couldn't help but feel a little giddy, to be honest.

I asked, "Are you Mr. Wills?" Nothing. "Do you know Mr. Wills?"

We heard a long drawn out "Yessssss."

"Is Mr. Wills here in the building?" I asked.

"Yes."

"Can we talk to him?"

A short burst of "No!" came next. I started to ask a question when we heard "He's with us." However, it wasn't over the speaker; it was in the room. Greg quickly turned the ghost box off.

I asked, "Why can't he speak with us?"

Nothing.

We asked more questions, but got no responses. After about fifteen minutes of dead silence, the room felt different, as if whatever was entertaining us had left.

We had about thirty minutes until sunrise, so we decided to move to the bar area, nervous about what may happen in the short amount of time before the sun rose. You know the old saying: it gets darkest before the dawn. Well, that's what the building started to feel like. It was almost as if it was tired and frustrated with us. The feeling in the building was heavy, a feeling I couldn't remember having felt before. It felt like, at any moment, a bomb would go off. We all could feel it. It felt claustrophobic, so much so that I almost called off the investigation, but something told me to keep pushing forward. We were almost done.

We entered the bar area, or at least what was left of it. All that remained was a large bar and a couple of old bar stools with a broken mirror hanging behind the bar. I walked to the bar and asked for a drink with no response, of course. Next thing I knew, Greg whipped out his trusted ghost box. Before I could even say no, he turned it on. *Here we go again*, I thought, but I was a little more open-minded because of the responses we got from Mr. Wills's room.

I asked, with a sarcastic tone, "What's a guy got to do around here to get a drink?" A female voice came over the ghost box and told me, "Go f*** yourself."

I quickly responded with, "You first!"

We then got another answer that told me, "Get the f*** out of here, now."

"Why are you being so nasty to me?" I asked.

The response that came through said, "Leave now motherf***er."

I looked at the other three as they picked their jaws off the floor and said, "We should probably leave now."

After I said that, I stopped and thought for a moment: *I'm not going anywhere until I get more answers.* I told everyone to stay seated; I needed some questions answered and I hoped this entity would keep responding to us. I asked, "What did you mean when you said to believe when we were downstairs? If that wasn't you downstairs, who was it? And can you ask them what they met by that?" Silence filled the room. All the cursing and foulmouthed insults went quiet as the static on the ghost box went flat. I walked around the room as if I was addressing a packed house in some auditorium.

"Who was speaking to us downstairs?" I asked one more time, hoping to get a response, but all was quiet. It was as if they were afraid to answer my questions.

I continued the questioning: "The one downstairs, is he the alpha? Is he in charge? Is that why you're afraid to answer for him?"

Several seconds passed before a soft-spoken voice came over the ghost box and answered with a yes.

"Yes, he's the boss? The one who is in charge? Is that what you are telling me, he's in charge? What's his name and why did he say *believe* to us?" I asked.

Once again all was quiet for several minutes. We were waiting for something to happen, and the room felt really tense and full of energy. It was very unsettling and uncomfortable in the room. Suddenly, a voice came over the ghost box and said, "Entering!"

At that point, my three colleagues jumped up off the floor as if expecting someone to barge through the door. Quite honestly, I had the same reaction, but I wasn't going to be the first to admit it.

All four of us stood there and stared at the doorway, waiting for something to appear or happen. It felt as if the seconds had turned into minutes as we waited. You could hear a pin drop as we stood in silence. All was quiet until I asked who or what was entering the room. Once again, a voice came over the ghost box. However, this time it was a woman's voice that we had not heard before. She sounded older and had a clearer, Southern-style accent compared to the voice we had heard earlier. It sounded as if the voice said "He will!"

Usually I'm hesitant to use ghost boxes because it can be a little tricky to hear the voices at times because they come across over white noise. A voice can also speak very fast and catch you off guard. That's the only way I can really explain the experience of using a ghost box to someone who has never used one of these devices before. As much as I don't like using ghost boxes in my investigations, something was different this time: I believed the answers that were coming from the device. There were way too many similarities between our questions and the responses we were receiving. It was one of the first times I felt as if I was able to carry on a conversation with someone who had passed on to the other side.

As we all stood and waited for our visitor to enter the room, we started to hear what sounded like hard-soled shoes walking nearby. It sounded as if the footsteps were coming closer, but then they would stop. This went on for several minutes until I approached the doorway to get a better perspective of the direction we were hearing them from. I stood in the doorway with my ear to the hallway listening for anything. Was this the same thing we encountered earlier when George was with us during the walk-through? Were these the same phantom footsteps that sent George into a panic thinking someone was in the building with us? As I listened, I started to hear what sounded like floor-boards creaking, as if someone or something was lingering outside the door. I quickly shined my flashlight through the doorway to see if I could catch a glimpse of what was making the sound I was hearing. I saw nothing except for my light cutting through the darkness. I stepped into the area where I heard the creaking sound and shined my light onto the floor to see if I could find anything that could have made that sound. Maybe it was an animal that made the sound.

Suddenly, something behind me took off running in the opposite direction. It startled me and I quickly turned around, slammed my hand into the door jamb, and dropped my flashlight. I grabbed the flashlight off the floor as fast as I could and pointed it in the direction I heard the running, but whatever it was, it was long gone. Without hesitation, I darted back into the room where the other three asked, frantically, what just happened. I told them what I heard but that I didn't see anything. They said they also heard something run away from where I was standing. Whatever had caused the sound left Greg and Stephanie ready to get out of there. I had to agree with them. It was time to go, plus it was almost daylight outside and a new day was upon us, along with a long day of travel back home for Keith and me.

I remember thinking to myself before leaving the room that what we just experienced was most likely not the alpha of the entities, but one of its followers or a lower-ranking member of the community that these entities had built there. I don't think it knew what to make of us yet and wasn't sure of our abilities or our strengths and weaknesses just yet. It seemed, to me, as if the alpha entity sent out a scout of sorts to feel us out just like it did when we first got there. I believed the entities we were talking to through the ghost box were probably of the "upper-middle class" in the world they created for themselves and that they felt threatened by us being there. In response to not knowing how to deal with us, these entities most likely reached out to the alpha to have us removed. In return, as a smart leader, this alpha sent out a lower-ranking follower to probe the situation and to report back what was going on. I think if we had stayed any longer, we would have pushed our luck. At some point, we might have woken the sleeping giant and had to deal with whatever it decided to bring to our investigation. I am glad we never got to that point.

We hastily made our way out of the room and down the stairs to the main apartment area. We all agreed it was time to start packing up. We filed out the door one at a time, with me bringing up the rear. I stopped for a moment in the apartment as I felt the presence of the sun breaking over the Cleveland skyline and across my shoulders. I turned and stared at it as if I'd never seen anything so beautiful before. Its amber-red midsummer haze shined across my face and at that point I knew we had survived the night. The first morning light has a way of making everything look alive and beautiful, even that old, decaying wicked place. I admired the House of Wills's beauty for a brief moment, then remembered what that building really was and decided it was time to go.

I finally made it to base camp with the others (see page 174). They looked the happiest I had seen them all night. I was pretty stoked as well to leave, get on the road, and wash my soul of this location. Keith and I still had eight hours of driving ahead of us, but it felt good to leave the House of Wills behind and get back to our families.

We all packed as fast as we could to get out and breathe the fresh air outside those doors. We got all our gear packed into the hard cases and loaded into the cars in record time, only because we started throwing the equipment in without a care in the world. I locked the side door with the key George gave us before he left and placed it in the secret hiding place. We piled into our cars and left the parking lot. I couldn't help but feel relief to leave the place, and everyone else seemed to feel the same way. As we made the turn to take us out of the city, I felt as if I had left a part of myself there and replaced it with a part of the House of Wills. I had a feeling that things would never be the same again from that day on.

Chapter 10

The Follower

We all stopped for breakfast at a diner near the outskirts of Cleveland to refuel and recap what happened over the past thirteen hours in a safe location. I didn't even know what to say about that place. With a grin on his face, Greg said, "I told you it was crazy." I said it would have been nice to know the owner was a member of a satanic church, and Keith blurted out, "Right!" Greg said he didn't know all that either. We scarfed down our breakfast as if we hadn't eaten solid food in weeks and payed our bills to our ever-happy waitress. In the parking lot, we bid our farewells with hugs and handshakes, until next time.

I drove the first leg of the drive home. Even though I had just eaten and not slept for over twenty-four hours, I had gotten a second wind and was ready to get home. The first hour, Keith and I talked nonstop about all the experiences we had during the investigation and how the location had been our most active place yet. About an hour and a half into our journey home, the sleep deprivation kicked in. Keith had fallen asleep in the passenger seat, but I fought to stay awake. All I needed to do was get to the halfway point and it was his turn. I was doing good until we hit the Pennsylvania line and the road became long and straight. All I kept thinking was *Come on! I've got this. Another two and a half hours, that's all.*

My warning sign to pull over was when I woke up from the noise from the rumble strips on the side of the road. I jerked awake and pulled the car back onto the highway. Keith jumped awake, poor guy. I nearly killed us both being stubborn and thinking I could make it that long without sleep. Keith talked to me until the next rest stop, which was thankfully about seven miles away.

We made it to the rest stop and I set my phone alarm for two hours. We both needed sleep and we still had a long way to go. After what seemed like minutes, the alarm went off and we settled back into our drive. At the halfway point, Keith took over to drive us the remaining four hours home. I could feel home getting closer by the mile, but I couldn't help but feel like something wasn't right. As Keith drove, I kept looking to the back seat as if I was going to say something to someone, but no one was there. I felt the presence of a child behind me. Keith asked what I was doing, and I told him I kept feeling like someone was in the back seat watching us. He said he had been feeling the same way since we left the House of Wills. When I asked him what it felt like, he said it felt like a kid sitting in the back seat watching us. For those of you that have children, when they are young and in a car seat, every so often you glance in the rearview mirror to see what they are doing in the back seat and they look back at you at the same time. That's what this sensation felt like, someone or something watching our every move. It was quite unsettling.

We were almost there, forty-five minutes from home, but we still had our possible follower or hitchhiker in the back seat. At this point, we could really feel the presence as we both kept looking behind us. Maybe it was lack of sleep or maybe it was because we had both been on edge for the last thirty-plus hours. We started chalking it up to everything we could to get our minds off it. We finally crossed the Delaware line and were minutes from Keith's house. We pulled into his driveway and all I could think of was that I was next to get home. I was just about to jump into the driver's seat when I saw that Keith had left some papers in the back seat. I yelled to him that he forgot something, but he said it was mine. I flipped it over and it was posters from Dr. King's march in Cleveland. Apparently, Greg and Stephanie had taken some of the old flyers from the attic and given them to Keith as a souvenir. I told him I didn't want them and he said neither did he, so I threw them in his outside garbage can.

I'm not big on bringing things home from locations I've investigated. I believe in attachments to material items and I don't want anything to follow me home. I still wonder if that's what we felt on our drive back. It's hard to say, but it could have been something attached to the flyer.

I got back in the car and went down the highway to my house. I still had about a twenty minute drive ahead of me, but at that point it was nothing compared to how long we had already been on the road. I decided I should probably have a conversation with my friend in the back seat before I got home. I started by saying, "Whoever you are, I have complete respect for you, but you are not allowed to follow me home or to cause any harm to me or my family. You need to go back to the House of Wills where you belong." I felt a little bit better.

Finally, I was home sweet home. I sat in my car for a minute or so because I was so happy to be back. I grabbed my gear and headed into the house to drop off the equipment in my office, say hi to the family, and get some sleep.

I headed upstairs to find my wife and kids to say hello, but the house was quiet. Not a whisper. I passed through the living room at the top of the stairs, and I saw no one. It was three in the afternoon on a Sunday so I expected someone to be in the house. I glanced into the kitchen; once again, nothing. I went down the hallway to see my youngest son Aaron's door closed. I put my ear to the door to see if I could hear him. At the time he was only three years old, so I didn't want to wake him from a nap by opening the door. I walked into my room to find Melanie asleep on the bed. I didn't want to wake her, so I decided to take a nap on the couch for an hour or so. All I remember is laying my head down and I was out like a light. The last two days had finally caught up with me. I woke to the sound of my seventeen-year-old son, Beck, stomping through the living room like a typical teenager. I grabbed my phone off the coffee table. It was five in the afternoon, on the dot. I had slept two hours but it felt like ten.

I went into the kitchen and found a note from my wife that said she and Aaron went to her parents for a little while and they would be home around eight. I felt really good, like I had slept for days, and my energy was through the roof. I had at least three or four hours of daylight left and it was beautiful outside. I had the bright idea it was time to clean the gutters. That's right, the guy with only two hours sleep was going to climb a ladder the height of a two-story house to clean the gutters. As I was in the garage pulling out my extension ladder, my son came in to ask what I was doing. I told him I was going to clean the gutters, and when he offered to help, I told him he could hold the ladder for me.

This is where it got weird for both of us. The next thing I remembered was sitting on the roof watching the sunset. I snapped out of my daze and headed over to the ladder and looked down. I didn't see Beck anywhere. As a father, I was worried and furious at the same time. I asked him one thing: to hold the ladder. I climbed down the ladder, went into the house, and yelled for him. He finally came downstairs and asked, "What's up?" I asked him why he stopped holding the ladder for me. He looked at me as if I had two heads. He said, "Dad, you told me you didn't need my help anymore."

I had no memory of that and told him I had just been up there for a few minutes. Beck told me that had been two hours ago. I quickly pulled my phone out to see that it read

8:00 p.m. Beck asked if I was okay and if I was mad at him. I told him I wasn't mad at him and that I was fine.

I walked back outside and saw leaf debris all over the ground where I cleaned the gutters. I took a seat on the lawn chair on the patio and tried my hardest to remember the last few hours. I had been on the roof for three hours and literally couldn't remember any of it. I couldn't even recollect climbing up the ladder. *Okay, I was just tired*, I thought to myself. It had been a crazy couple of days. I needed to eat and get some rest, that's all.

I pulled the ladder down and started to put it back in the garage. I wanted to get the mess cleaned up before Melanie and Aaron got home. As I put the ladder back on the wall of the garage, I heard what sounded like buzzing behind me. At first, I thought it was coming from the fridge in the garage. I turned around to go check out the fridge, and what I saw next was straight out of a 1970s horror movie.

It's hard to put into words what I witnessed that day in my garage. When I turned around and actually saw what was making the buzzing sound, I stopped in my tracks and couldn't believe my eyes. What I saw covering the two double windows facing the front yard shook me to the bone. Hundreds of blackflies covered the windows. There were so many of them they nearly blocked out the light from the outside. Beck entered the garage from the house and also saw them. I quickly grabbed the first can of bug spray I could find on the shelf and told Beck to leave as I started spraying them. I started to choke from the fumes and had to leave the garage immediately. I slammed the door shut behind me and locked it. Beck was standing behind me in the hallway that leads into the downstairs den. He asked me where all those flies came from. I told him I didn't know and then walked outside to get some air.

Just as I walked out the back door, Melanie and Aaron pulled around the back of the house to park. I quickly gained my composure and greeted them with big hugs. I hoped Melanie didn't notice how shaken I was by what I just saw in the garage. I needed to keep her out of there until I could get it cleaned up and figure out what was going on.

I know what you are thinking. This sounds like something from a movie. I agree, it does, and it's the first thing that went through my mind. This only happens in horror films. But God as my witness, this really happened, but at the time I wasn't convinced myself. There had to be a rational explanation for all of this. I waited until the two of them retreated upstairs then I reentered the garage to see what damage I had inflicted on the infestation.

The room was still full of mist from the spray and the fumes were still strong. I covered my face with my shirt and approached the windows to see hundreds of flies covering the floor and windowsills. Most were dead but a few still twitched about on the floor. I cleaned it up right away soas not to raise suspicion if someone else were to see it. I swept up the evidence and discreetly disposed of it in the outside trash can. I told myself not panic, it was just flies. But then I started to think. I never had anything like that happen ever in our house until now, and the fact that I just got back from that horrible place didn't help. I kept telling myself to calm down and that it was all in my head.

I went to bed early that night and thankfully slept very soundly. When my alarm went off at five in the morning, I had almost forgotten what had happened the night before. As I sat on the couch drinking coffee while the sun rose from across the cornfield in front of my house, it hit me. The flies! I jumped up to check and make sure all was well in the garage. I slowly walked downstairs to the garage door. I stood there for a moment with my hand on the handle. I thought to myself, *Please, Lord, don't let there be any more flies*. I repeated that several times before I turned the handle.

I opened the door and reached for the light. What was I going to do if they were back? The light illuminated the bright white walls of the room. And like that, nothing. No buzzing, no flies, not even the sound of the occasional cricket. I was so relieved and happy. I felt as if it was all just bad timing for the most part. I went back up to finish my coffee and breakfast so I could start my day, thinking to myself, *It's a new day. I'm confident. Let's do this!*

I had a few minutes before I had to go to work, so I decided to put my equipment away in the office before I left. As I opened the office door, something was off. I could feel it, like a sixth sense of sorts. Then, I heard the sound of buzzing. There were flies covering my office windows. I felt like I was struck with vertigo; a feeling of dizziness flushed over my entire body. I rushed to the garage and grabbed what was left of the spray, ran back into the room, and filled it with bug spray. I left the room and shut the door behind me. *This can't be happening*, I thought to myself. *There is no way; not again. Damn it! What can I do, who can I call? This is insane. I'm losing my mind. What if something did follow me home? How do I get it out, and how do I protect my family from it?* I didn't care if an entity messed with me. But mess with my family? I draw the line there. How could I protect my family from something that I couldn't see and was not of flesh and blood? These are all the things that raced through my mind that day. I started making calls and sending text messages on my way to work. I tried to reach out to people I knew in the field who could help or tell me what to do next. I'd never experienced anything like this in all my years investigating. My mind was going a thousand miles an hour and still not getting anywhere. The day at work took forever. I couldn't concentrate or focus on any of my duties. I needed to get home to protect my family at all costs. I still had not told Melanie what I thought was going on, and I hoped I could fix it before she found out.

Chapter 11

Oppression

I sat at my desk at work that day and gazed into the void of my computer screen. I couldn't snap out of it. I was not myself. At the time, I held a very important management position with a company. Dozens of subcontractors counted on me to be their middleman for customers who were spending tens of thousands of dollars on renovations to their homes. I had to fix what was going on at home so I could get back to normal at my job. If not, things would just get worse. All I could do was question what had I done, what did I bring home with me, and how do I fix it? I had never dealt with anything like this and had just catapulted myself into a true-life horror story with no end in sight. I felt hopeless and defeated, but I couldn't give up, if not for me but my family. They didn't deserve whatever came home with me. They weren't the ones that went to the House of Wills unprepared and let this thing, this entity, into our lives.

The clock on my computer could not move fast enough. I needed to go, and I needed to go now. I quicky put together a group email and sent it out to all the contractors that worked under me. I said I was leaving the office for the rest of the day and to forward any work orders to my underwriter in the office. I told the poor kid who worked under me I had to go and ran out the door without giving him any reason. God knows what he thought at the time, but I honestly did not care.

I raced home hoping to beat everyone else there. The drive that time of day could be long because of traffic, but I had to try my best. I blew through every yellow light that got in my way. Thank the traffic gods I made it home before everyone. I needed to check the office and the garage first thing. I opened the office door. Nothing. No buzzing, no flies. I walked into the garage and all was quiet. I searched the rest of the house, top to bottom. Nothing was found, not even a trace of a fly or any other insect.

I checked my phone to see if anyone had gotten back to me. Two people I knew and trusted in the field responded. Both of them told me the same thing: I needed to cleanse the house with sage, but they each told me different ways of doing it. Who was right, or were they both wrong, and where was I going to get sage? I then remembered Stephanie gave Keith and me sage when we were at the House of Wills. I ran downstairs to my office and started going through my cases. I blew it off at the time, but damn it, I needed it. I found the sage under my LED lights, right where I put it. Just kidding, I literally just tossed it in my case thinking I would throw it out once I got home.

Just as I went to light the sage and follow the instructions given to me, I heard Melanie pull up. *Okay, this can wait until later, I hope*, I thought to myself. I hid the sage in my office until later, hoping nothing would kick off before then. The night dragged by as I watched the clock tick, minute by minute, like a child waiting for Christmas morning. Eventually it became clear I would get to the cleansing that night. I would have to go into work late the next day and do it after everyone left the house in the morning.

Melanie could feel the tension between me and what was going on, but at the same time knew nothing of what was going on in the house or to what extent the stress of it was having on me mentally and physically. I was able to hide it well—at least I thought so at the time. As for my son Beck, I was able to dismiss the flies in the garage as a freak onetime experience that I easily brushed off to cover my tracks. I was very lucky that neither of them had any experiences as I did. Whatever followed me back from that godforsaken place was feeding off me and I had its full attention because I was the one who trespassed on its domain. I was also the one who opened myself up to it and fed it the attention it desired, which in turn made it stronger. If I hadn't taken control of it when I did, I'm sure it would have eventually moved to other members of my family.

I went to bed that night with a glimmer of hope that I might be able to turn this around and fix the mess I brought home with me. I thought back to the night of the investigation when something tried to attach itself to me in the basement of the building. I knew at that point whatever that was wasn't good, and I should have left when it happened to me. But with my inexperience and alpha male bullheadedness, I stayed at the House of Wills. All of this happened because I didn't want to back down from something that, at the time, I thought was weak and a joke. If I learned anything from my mistakes, it was that I needed to humble myself and take a different path as an investigator or get out of the paranormal field altogether. This stuff is real, and up to the point of me walking through those doors and into that building in Cleveland, I had only scraped the very surface with a few EVPs and a picture of some shadow anomaly here or there. Whatever I had encountered at the House of Wills was the real deal and it meant business. I needed to stand up and fight back or chance losing everything that I knew, loved, and had built in my life. I was not going to let that happen. It was going to have to kill me before I let it win. I knew one thing: it wasn't going to break my will to fight back. I would give this fight everything I had in me to beat it.

I was in bed, staring at the ceiling, waiting to fall asleep. I looked at the clock every twenty minutes as I tossed and turned, waiting for sleep to come. This went on for several hours. My eyes were fully adjusted to the darkness of the room when I suddenly noticed something had changed. The room had gotten darker and it felt as if someone was watching me from the master bathroom. Suddenly, the motion sensor night-light came on from inside the bathroom. I watched the door that lead into the bathroom and waited to catch a glimpse of whatever triggered the night-light. But then the light turned off and the room became even darker as I waited for something to happen.

My eyes focused on a dark mass that was darker than the rest of the room. I watched as it moved from the door-way and across the room and stood next to the windows that face the backyard. I surprisingly wasn't scared. I was more captivated by what it was and why it was there. I got my nerve up and asked out loud, "Who are you?" It quickly darted from the windows, back across the room, and through the bedroom door. I jumped out of bed and went into the hallway and hoped I could see where it went.

I walked into the kitchen and turned on the light, almost blinding myself. I was starting to get worried. Where did it go? Did it go into one of my kids'rooms? Was it hiding some-where else in the house, or did it just leave? I honestly didn't know, and at that point my eyes were not adjusted to the dark so I probably wouldn't be able to see it again that night. All I knew was that morning couldn't come quick enough.

I sat on the couch with the kitchen light on, hoping to catch sight of it again, until I eventually fell asleep. I woke up at first light with the sounds of the garbage truck picking up our trash. *Why do they come so damn early?* I thought to myself as I got up and stumbled into the kitchen to make coffee. Soon the house would be filled with the sounds of kids rushing around, getting ready for school, and demand-ing breakfast.

I waited for my moment. Finally, everyone was off to school or work. It was time to take back my house. I carefully read the two text messages that I received the day before. I grabbed the sage from the office and lit it, not having a clue what I was doing or if it would even work, but something was better than not trying at all. I followed the instructions to the letter. I went through every space in the house: the closets, the attic, the laundry room, you name it. An hour later, I was done and the house smelled like white sage. I hoped it would air out by the time everyone got home. I took a shower and got ready to head out to work. The house definitely felt different. It felt lighter and not as heavy. I headed to work that day feeling good, like everything was behind me now and my family was safe.

The day flew by at work, and I couldn't wait to get home to see everyone and relaxe. That evening went by quickly, like many do, and it was time for bed. My son Aaron wanted to lie in bed with me and watch his shows on his Kindle until he fell asleep. Melanie decided to stay up and catch up on her shows, so Aaron and I turned in. I started to fade off while watching my three-year-old boy laughing and enjoying his cartoons. It was one of the moments you can never get back and brings joy to your heart seeing your kid's smile while you watch from a distance.

I was just getting ready to close my eyes when I noticed him peeking over his Kindle, looking toward the bathroom door. This caught my attention quickly as I followed his line of sight and looked where he was staring. I saw nothing, but he did, and he ducked his head under the covers. Anger took over as I thought to myself, *You can mess with me all you want, but don't mess with my kids, you son of a bitch.* I didn't want to scare Aaron any more than he already was, so I calmed myself and pulled him closer to me until he eventually fell asleep in my arms as I thought, *Whoever or whatever you are, now it's war!*

The next day came quickly, and I felt my mood change from happy-go-lucky to mad and ready to snap. I couldn't get the look of fear on my son's face out of my head, and it angered me more and more by the moment. How dare this entity follow me home, trespass on my property, and scare my family. I did some research that morning to try to find someone who could help me. I got lots of responses from friends and peers in the field and tried multiple things with no luck. The feeling in the house was heavy to me. I still hadn't told Melanie at this point, but I could see our moods changing toward each other. I felt myself losing my drive, and for the first time in my life that I could remember, I felt true depression. My thoughts were getting darker by the day and my mood swings were becoming more noticeable, even at work. I was almost to the point where I was starting to embrace it. It was becoming a part of me. By the second week, I was completely depressed and sick. I wasn't eating, I had no energy, and I didn't even want to get out of bed in the mornings. I wasn't noticing anything anymore. It was as if the days were going by while I drifted through them. In my head I wanted to fight back, but I couldn't even get the energy up to care anymore. I was lost at this point and I had nowhere to turn.

The month of August was upon us, and I was tired, sick, and ready to give up. It had been almost four weeks since the investigation at the House of Wills. Things were quiet around the house for a few days. It was late in the evening of August 5. I was sitting in the rocking chair in the living room, watching television, when a strange feeling came over me. Out of the corner of my eye, I noticed movement on the bookshelves next to where I was sitting. I turned to see a large vase on the shelf rocking from side to side. Then it started to spin like if you dropped a coin on the floor. I quickly got up to grab it before it fell off the shelf and it stopped dead. I picked it up to look inside and see if there was a mouse or a battery-operated toy inside and found nothing. I felt that whatever was there in the house was letting me know it was still there.

Several more days passed and the activity in my house started to increase again. I sat for several nights and watched a shadow figure (or shadow anomaly, as I like to call them) go from the hallway to the kitchen. I saw this happen more than a dozen times. I can only imagine how many other times it occurred when no one saw it. I'd grown used to the activity, which wasn't good or fair to my family, who were the real victims in all of this. I went to the House of Wills and got myself into this. I had tried everything that I knew of and reached out to dozens of people in the field. They all tried to help and suggested a lot of things but none of them worked

I layed in my bed, silent, waiting for something to happen. It felt like waiting for a bomb to go off. It was nerve-racking and exhausting. The whole experience wore me down. I was almost to the point of no return. Out of nowhere, I said out loud, "God, why me?" Up to this point, I was not the praying type. I believed in a higher power and everything, but religion wasn't my thing. I hadn't said a prayer since I was a kid. I was raised to recite the "Now I lay me down to sleep and pray my lord my soul to keep" every night as a child.

I decided this starts now. I am fighting back, not just for me, but for my family. I jumped out of bed and had no idea where to start. Do I get down on my knees and start asking for help or what? I argued with myself for twenty minutes on how to pray. It was pathetic. I'm sure God took mercy on me for being so bad at it. I got on my knees and asked for help in every way I could think of at the time. This went on for a good ten minutes until I felt that I did my best work and hoped a miracle would occur. I went to bed with a new-found confidence that night.

The next morning came and I felt a little better than before. Maybe it was all in my head, but I wasn't so sure. I was still waiting for a bomb to go off at any moment. I felt like I was walking on eggshells, trying not to get my hopes up. The day passed without incident. Okay, maybe I was on to something. That night I repeated more prayers and did it again the following night.

Nothing happened for the next three days, and I was honestly starting to feel like myself again. I kept this same routine up for a week and felt better each day until it became a habit for me. Up to this very day, six years later, I still pray twice a day and thank God for all he has blessed me with in my life. I am not a church-going person and there is nothing wrong with church. It helps a lot of people every day to get through their problems and give them hope and a place to worship. But I also believe everyone can pray and worship God, or whomever they worship, from their own homes in the way they want to.

I do believe prayers helped me and my family. I believe whatever was in my home was dark and evil, and me finding God, or whatever you want to call it, drove it off and back to wherever it came from. I guess you can say the House of Wills made me a God-fearing man. Maybe that's what I needed in my life at the time. I was cocky and stubborn as a paranormal investigator and this experience humbled me as a man. But in doing that, it made me stronger and who I am today as an investigator but more importantly as a man. I look back on it today in this very moment and thank God for it happening to me. I wouldn't change it for anything at this point. It's made me a better, more rounded person in life in general. And it has opened my eyes up to so much more in this field of the paranormal.

I most likely would not have experienced this if not for that night I spent in the House of Wills. I don't recommend anyone going out to look for these kinds of places. My time in that building was a complete coincidence. I don't know, but I warn you, especially you folks out there who are new at this. Do not go looking for trouble. These places, such as the House of Wills, exist. They are real and dangerous to the most experienced of investigators. If you decide to investigate a location like this and do not take my warning, you need to be ready for the worst. Keep your baggage at home, and I don't mean the material kind. If you are having family or financial problems, or if you're sick or not feeling good mentally or physically, stay away by all means. These types of places feed off that negativity. You have been warned!

Chapter 12

Slow Burn

Once things calmed down at home, I was able to reflect on my time at the House of Wills and what I thought happened there and what exists there. What I am getting ready to tell you is complete speculation and theory on my part. I came up with this theory because of my time and experience after the investigation. I have spent countless hours studying the paranormal and investigating all over this country on and off the show *Ghost Hunters*. I have spent time at some of the most infamous and haunted locations known to man. With that said, I believe the House of Wills is what some of us in the field call a slow burn, which is when the activity slowly builds over many years and experiences. It keeps growing, feeding off energy, and can result in some rather explosive and powerful paranormal activity. I also believe what is happening there is most likely in part man-made.

The reason I say that is because before Eric took over ownership of the building, it was a peaceful location according to Patty. Don't get me wrong, it had its share of bad apples over the years, and it all can't be blamed on Eric. I believe the negative energy in the building to be combination of events that happened there. There has been some tragic history that has happened there over the countless years. Numerous murders and violent acts had taken place on the property over the years, due to the fact it's in a rough area of East Cleveland. I also think the many purposes the building served and the people tied to affected it's energy. The architect was a high-degree mason, it was a German social club, reported to be a speakeasy during Prohibition, and Cleveland's largest African American funeral home.

I have come across a few slow burns over the years. In my opinion, the House of Wills is the biggest one yet. I believe it's a powder keg just waiting for a spark to ignite it. There are all the right ingredients for it. All the different hats it has worn, all those years it was a funeral home and a place of worship, its downfall in the mid-2000s, and now one of the high priests of the new satanic church owns it. So many different types of energy, residual or intelligent, good and bad, all piled on top of each other. It is the perfect paranormal storm.

I mean no disrespect to Eric or anyone else who was a part of this once amazing location. To each their own, and I believe that Eric means well. He's put a lot of money, time, effort, blood, and sweat into the House of Wills to save it, and still does to this very day. But with the spirits that were already there, if most of them were from a Christian background and then you bring in the opposite of that, those energies collide. This is how a slow burn starts.

I don't want to think it was started on purpose. If it was, I don't think it was Eric who started it. It could have been someone else with ill intentions, not to mention the countless paranormal teams coming and going year after year. I have been in this field for quite a while and I have seen what some of these guys do. For the record, 99.9 percent of paranormal teams are just there to have fun and do things right. I am speaking of that 0.1 percent who are there to taunt the spirits and do rituals they have no business doing.

A slow burn survives as it feeds off human energy, like it did with me, by taking little pieces over time to keep its fire burning until one day it's a raging inferno you can't control. That's exactly what it's doing. I have spoken to multiple people who investigated at the House of Wills before and after me who had very similar experiences. I believe what came home with me was not so much an entity but an actual piece of the location. I felt like when I left that morning, I had swapped a piece of me for a piece of it.

I believe there are other things going on there. I spoke earlier of a community of souls. That is what happens when a building or a house is vacant for many years. Sometimes there are one or two spirits already at the location, and others are invited or wander in over time. In the case of the House of Wills, I think its entity community consists of Mr. Wills, those who frequented the location when it was a club, or those whose funerals were held there; the possibilities are quite extensive of who might be hanging around there. When you bring in a darker side of things, it attracts darker energies, spirits, and possibly nonhuman spirits. My theory is that they have taken over, are running the show, and are possibly holding human spirits hostage in the location. That is why what was once a peaceful place where the spirits were at rest changed not long after Eric took over the building. Opinions vary on this, but I stand by my theory.

This story of the House of Wills has been well covered and documented by the local media in Cleveland and several podcasts, including my own back in 2017 when I interviewed Eric about the House of Wills and his beliefs.

During the interview, I perceived Eric as a very intelligent man who just happened to have a different belief system than most people. He said he did not believe in the afterlife or the paranormal. But he admitted he had seen full-body apparitions in the building while living there. He personally witnessed one walk across a room, right in front of him, in broad daylight. When I asked why he did not believe in spirits or the afterlife, even after seeing it firsthand on several occasions, he implied he could not explain what he saw. Just because he saw it doesn't make it real to him, and he shuts it off and doesn't think about it, especially because at the time of the interview he was living in the building.

Eric also told us the reason why he finally went public about his beliefs. Eric and his girlfriend had moved into the building to be closer to the property so it would be easier for him to work on the building and renovate it at his leisure, as well as deter recent acts of vandalism against the building and surrounding property. A local outspoken leader of the community made accusations that all the evil events happening in East Cleveland, such as drive-by shootings and murders, were due to the House of Wills and the things going on behind closed doors in the building. The local community was riled up to rally against Eric.

Over several weeks, Eric received threats from this community leader and some of the locals who were heading this witch hunt and fueled the fire against Eric. After multiple threats and vandalism did not work to scare Eric, they decided to step it up a notch and put their words into action. One night while Eric and his girlfriend were in their apartment in the building, several armed men broke down the front door of the property to hunt Eric and his girlfriend down. Eric had built a safe room where he and his girlfriend could hide, since he suspected this very thing might happen. The armed intruders couldn't find them and were getting angrier by the moment, so they decided to burn the place down and be done with it. With gas cans in hand, they decided to start the fire in the auditorium since that was the largest room in the building. They doused the large wooden statues as well as several other parts of the room with gasoline and lit it on fire in hopes the entire building would burn to the ground. After the room was on fire, they fled the scene of the crime.

THE LARGE WOODEN STATUES WERE DAMAGED IN A FIRE CAUSED BY VANDALS

After Eric knew the coast was clear, he and his girlfriend escaped and were able to call for help. Fortunately, the only things that burned were the statues. The rest of the building was unharmed by the blaze. It's strange to think that after the room was set on fire, the only things that burned were the demonic medieval-type statues that Eric hand-carved and brought into the building. It surprised me that this tinder box of a building did not burn down. When I was there, the place was decaying and rotten wood was everywhere. It blows my mind that it's still standing after that event.

After all this happened, the entire story of what was going on in that neighborhood with the community and Eric was leaked to the media. It became front page news in Cleveland, and local news stations got involved. After no one was brought to justice for the attempted murders and arson, the media was able to get both sides of the story. They brought Eric and the community leader who was leading the witch hunt together in a meeting to sit down, talk, and hash out their differences. Eric said they were able to come to a truce of sorts and work things out. I don't know the details of this meeting, but whatever they were, it stopped all the threats and attempts on Eric and the location.

This story is just another chapter in the long history of this building. This is another example of the slow burn I spoke of earlier. What would possess someone to stay there after all that, and why did the community decide that all the crime in that neighborhood was caused by one person or a building? The House of Wills is like a moth to a flame. It draws in energy, and not always the good kind.

Chapter 13

The Revisit

Six months after the investigation at the House of Wills, I finally got back into investigating. I needed to take some time off and get healthy again after visiting the House of Wills, both mentally and physically. After those six months of healing, I felt great. It was winter and the weather sucked, but I still felt good. I was asked to lead my team, consisting of Keith, Greg, and Stephanie, on a three-day paranormal adventure through Ohio. We had become regular paranormal running mates to all these insane locations during our journeys.

Three different locations in three days? Hell, why not? It had been a while and I felt better prepared spiritually than ever before. We went to Cincinnati first, to an infamous haunted location that is supposedly off the charts with paranormal activity. The investigation went well, and we had some great moments, but it was nothing compared to what we went through six months earlier at the House of Wills.

After a long night of investigating and very little rest, we were off to our next spot, not far from Columbus, Ohio. We spent the day investigating and once again had a great time there, but it paled in comparison to the House of Wills. I felt like I was chasing that first high. What I experienced at the House of Wills was a once-in-a-lifetime event, and, quite honestly, I never wanted to go through that again.

We headed to our third and final spot about forty-five minutes north of Cleveland. I knew we had to skirt Cleveland to get to where we were going, but once I saw we were actually heading into the city, I knew something was up. The streets started to look familiar. I asked Greg where were we going. He laughed and said he texted Patty and that she would meet us at the House of Wills to walk through the building. I told him he was an ass and that I was never going back there. He said it would just be for a little bit. I told him no. I wasn't going in. I remember heading down East 55th Street and feeling the building getting closer. As we pulled into the parking lot, my hands were shaking. Everyone hopped out of the SUV except me. When Greg asked if I was coming in, I told him, "What did you not understand about what I said?" I sat in the car like a child pouting over not getting a toy. After thirty-five minutes had passed, I noticed we had drawn the attention of the locals as they stared from the apartment building across the way. This wasn't good. I sat silently for several more minutes and a feeling of anger rushed over me. I thought, *The hell with this. I need to face*

my fears. This place isn't going to beat me. I got out of the
SUV and walked up to the side door that was open. When
we were here before, it was boarded shut and had chains
and padlocks on it. I walked in and stepped over the threshold. The feeling of uneasiness came over me.

I looked to the top of the landing and saw everyone standing there, amazed that I came in. Keith asked if I was good,
and I sarcastically said, yeah just fine, and looked in Greg's
direction. He said they were just leaving. Good. I told them
I'd be right back as I walked up the stairs to the second floor
(see page 174). I stared down the hallway into nothingness.
Under my breath I said, "You didn't beat me, you son of
bitch." I turned and walked back downstairs past everyone
and out the door. Soon everyone followed. We stood at the
side of the building under the overhang and talked to Patty
for about twenty minutes until we noticed the time and realized we had to get to our next location.

After we had left the building and were standing outside,
I asked Patty if things were the same or if anything changed
since our last visit to the location. She explained that things
were the same and groups were no longer allowed into the
building for overnight investigations. When I asked why, she
explained it had become too dangerous for the people visiting
and things had escalated with the local community. The place
has gotten worse for investigators and for people not experienced enough to deal with what can happen to them at the
House of Wills. Patty said she stopped visiting the building as
often as well.

I told her that it seemed lighter in the building compared to our previous visit. She laughed and said it was because she was there with us. I asked her what she meant by that, and she said the entities behave when she was there. Patty said the spirits were almost like her kids and they knew not to act up when she was around. She also added if we were there without her that we could have problems. I thanked her for taking the time out of her day to meet us there and to let us in the building. With a smile, she said we were more than welcome anytime as we said our goodbyes.

As we left Cleveland, I felt a sense of relief, as if I was able to finally close that chapter of my life and move forward. It felt good and I was glad we went and that I was able to do that. Before that moment, I swore I would never reenter that building.

We made it to our next location in good time. The investigation was a good one, with lots of experiences, but to be honest, we were all beat. We bit off way more than we could chew on this trip: three locations in less than seventy-two hours and a pit stop at the House of Wills. We wrapped early that night, around two in the morning, and left for home. Thankfully there was no hitchhiker with us this time.

Chapter 14

Devastation

I'm not sure if I was actually able to beat my demons or just learn how to control them. Even six years after visiting the House of Wills, I had a hard time writing this and it dug up some old memories I had buried deep down inside of me. I also found myself starting to slip back into those old feelings from back then. I quickly noticed the warning signs and was able to deter them by sheer will and prayer. To give everyone an example of the impact this place has on other people, not just me, during the second day of filming *Ghost Hunters,* I was working with the show's director of photography, Kendall. We were doing hero shots where you stand still, look all serious, and the photographer takes dozens of pictures as they move around you. They use them for promotional material. Kendall and I were making small talk, just getting to know each other while he was doing

143

his thing with the pictures. He asked me what the craziest location was that I had ever investigated. I immediately told him it was the House of Wills. Kendall immediately jumped up and asked if I had really said the House of Wills. I was puzzled at the time and asked if he had heard of it. He said he had and that the place is evil. Russ, one of the producers, chimed in from across the set and asked what we were talking about. When we told him, he said, "Dude that place is evil and I will never go back there."

They were both on a show prior to *Ghost Hunters* that filmed there. They both responded they had a hard time shaking the place and had vivid dreams for weeks after leaving.

Fast-forward several months and a few investigations later. At this point it's late in the summer of 2016. I was tired of running around to investigations and breaking the bank at the same time. For you out there who are reading this and are serious investigators, you know what I am talking about. Ghost hunting can get expensive quickly. Between all the equipment and location fees and travel, it's expensive, especially when you don't have a production company paying for all of it.

I was brainstorming a way I could stay in the paranormal field without leaving the comfort of my own home and not break the bank. A friend of mine mentioned I should try live streaming or podcasts. I was intrigued but knew nothing about running one or how to even start one. I had been on a few podcasts as a guest, but that's it. I saw an ad on social media from a small streaming site that was looking for a new show to broadcast from their network. What the hell, why not? I hit the guy up, we started talking, and I got the gig.

I had a couple of investigations lined up for the month of October and once they were done, I had an open schedule for the month of November to start my live stream. I had no idea what to expect out of this. I am not the most tech savvy person, although I'm much better these days. Back then we didn't have all the streaming apps like we do now. Everything was either Lookouts or OBS. It was not fun for a man who could barely copy and paste to host an hour-long show with a co-host, but I was determined to figure it out.

We were set to go live the Monday before Thanksgiving. The show was called *American Ghost Hunter*. I was so excited and we had some awesome guests lined up for the first couple episodes. But then everything in my life turned upside down in seconds. On the morning of November 14, 2016, at approximately eight in the morning, my life changed forever.

I had the morning off and didn't have to be into work until later that day. I was in my office doing some odds and ends when I noticed a county police officer slow down going past my house, stop, and back into my driveway. At first, I thought maybe he was turning around or was setting up a speed trap. I live on a back road and people love to speed up and down the road. Some of my neighbors complained about the speeding to the county and state due to the fact there had been a few bad accidents on that stretch of road. I thought nothing of it and went back to what I was doing as I could see the officer sitting in his SUV. I was all for having a speed trap out there and I welcomed them to use my driveway.

His door opened and he stepped out and started to walk toward the house. My driveway is pretty long so I thought I better go and meet him halfway to make sure everything was all right. I got up the steps and opened the door to head outside and he was already standing there, getting ready to knock. I opened the door to ask if I could help him and he had a somber expression on his face. He asked me if Nicholas Marston resided here. At first, I honestly didn't know what to say. I did not want to get my son in trouble so I said, "I'm his father. How can I help you, officer?" He then took a deep breath and asked again but this time his tone was different, like one father to another father. "Does he live here, Mr. Marston?" "Yes, officer. He does," I stated. He then began a sentence that to this very day haunts my soul and I hear repeated almost every day of my life in the back of my head. It's one thing no parent ever wants to hear. "I regret to inform you that your son, Nicholas Elijah Marston, was pronounced dead at 8:16 a.m. this morning by doctors at the hospital." I dropped to my knees before he was able to finish his sentence. If you ever want to know true pain, ask someone who has lost a child.

The loss of a child changes a person, whether for good or bad. It can break you forever or make you stronger. This is what I've learned about myself from the loss of Nicholas. Little things used to bother me, and honestly very little bothers me now. I've learned that I am numb and almost desensitized from the things in the outside world. I am now even more protective of my family and children than ever. I love life and I am intent on seeing the silver lining in almost every situation. On the other hand, I yearn for the day I can leave this world so I can be with my son again. I tell myself someday but not today. I still have things to do, but someday I'll see my kid again. This is what keeps me going every day of my life. Keeping myself busy with different projects in and outside of the paranormal field helps as well. I realize most days how blessed I have been in life and all the opportunities that have been bestowed on me, such as having a great family, healthy children, and a roof over our heads. The things so many of us take for granted every day. These are things you start to notice around you after a traumatic event. You notice the sunrises and sunsets more and how the setting sun cascades its light off that one tree in the backyard in the same spot every day. Or an orange autumn moon and the crisp smell of fall. Or the sounds of crickets on a summer's eve. These are the things I cherish now, knowing my son cannot anymore; I cherish them for him in his memory.

Chapter 15

Chance of a Lifetime

Several weeks had passed since we lost Nicholas and I was lost. My mind was going in a thousand different directions at once. I knew I had to do something to keep my mind off it, even if it was only for a couple hours a week. I decided we should move forward with the live stream and see how things went for a while. We literally only had about ten people watching for the first show, but that was not going to deter me. As the weeks and months went by, we gradually built our audience. It was exciting, and in a way, it was therapy for me and kept me busy in between work and home life. After a year and a half, I reached out to the big boys on the block of paranormal live streams and podcasts. Paranormal Warehouse was the largest of all the live stream networks at the time. They ran multiple shows with tens of thousands of viewers on all their shows. The shows ranged from paranormal talk to live psychic readings and live investigations. I didn't think we had a chance to get picked up, but it was worth a try. After about a week or so, I received an email that said they would love to have us join the network.

After we joined Paranormal Warehouse, our numbers went from a hundred or so people watching a week to thousands of people watching live. It was overwhelming at first, but it was also a lot of fun. We were just winging it. I believe our not being too serious about the subject matter or whatever guest we had on that week made us popular and relatable to most. We had a bit of a struggle finding guests for our early shows, but soon we had people lining up to be on our show. After several shows, we had to post a parental advisory banner at the beginning of the show due to our colorful language and material. We had become the bad boys of the network and it was a title I was honored to hold. I went through a few co-hosts at first, but then I assembled a team of co-hosts consisting of Greg Knepp (yes, the same Greg from the House of Wills investigation), who was based in Ohio, and Alex and Helena King, who were based in the UK. I was in Delaware.

I remember not being a big fan of all the paranormal television shows at the time. I felt as if they were just going in circles and had no direction at all. I also remember bashing them in a nice way on my show, if it's even possible to bash something or someone nicely. I shouted out to the paranormal gods almost every week that I would never be on a TV show.

One cold winter's night around 7 p.m., I was playing Nerf gun wars with my son Aaron. My phone rang and it was a phone number I didn't recognize from Burbank, California. I did what any normal person would do. I let it go to voice mail. I thought it was someone trying to tell me my car warranty had expired or something. When I received the notification I had a message, I laughed and wondered what it was they were selling. However, when I listened to the message, it was some producer from LA named Nick asking to have a meeting about some paranormal TV show.

After about two days of playing phone tag, I had a video meeting with some producers out of LA. I know what you're thinking: What happened to never wanting to be on a show? Quite honestly, I didn't think I had a chance in hell of getting it. Why not go through the motions and see what the process is like? It couldn't hurt, right?

The video meeting and everything went as I thought it would. They asked a bunch of questions in different ways and videotaped the whole meeting. I couldn't even see who I was speaking with, but they could see me. All that lasted about thirty minutes. The meeting ended and they said if they needed anything else, they would call me.

At that moment, I figured I didn't get the job and got up to tell Melanie how the meeting went. Suddenly, my phone rang. It was the producer Nick. He wanted to say the meeting went well and they'd like to offer a ninety-day contract. I asked what that meant, and he said until they make their final choice, they didn't want anyone else grabbing me up. I actually laughed out loud at that. I had the contracts in my email in less than five minutes. After several weeks of phone calls, emails, and more video meetings, they asked me to fly out to Burbank, California. The next thing I knew, I was on a flight to Burbank.

I sat in a room for about ten hours, taking tests and talking to two different psychologists as a third-party moderator sat between all of us. It was insane what you have to go through to get on TV. I get it now, but I never would have thought I had to go through all that for a show. Most of it is for insurance reasons and to make sure you're not some kind of nutcase. Even after all that, they sent me home after two days, and I still didn't know if I was hired or not.

On Friday I got a call that said I should know by Monday if they are going with me or not. Great, I'd have all weekend to think about it. Everything was going through my head. Did I answer all their questions correctly or did I say something wrong or did they find something in my social media they found questionable? For anyone out there hoping to get on a TV show, you better have a squeaky clean social media presence because if you don't, they will find it. They have a third-party company who does it for them, and they go all the way back to the beginning of every account you've ever had.

It was late Sunday night and I could not sleep a bit, plus there was a bad storm with thunder, lightning, and strong wind going on outside. All of a sudden, I heard a loud cracking sound from outside, but it was way too dark to see what the crack was. As I watched through the back dining room windows, the lighting lit up the backyard for a brief moment and I could see lighting had struck one of the big pine trees. It was split in half and laying in the backyard. I thought to myself, *Great, this can't be a good omen of things to come.*

The storm passed during the night, and when it was morning, I wanted to check out the damage and see if the tree needed to be cut down, but I had to get to work. It would have to wait. At the time, I was not working a nine-to-five job anymore. I owned a contracting business with a partner and we were in the middle of rebuilding a house that had a fire several months earlier. I was on a tight schedule to get these people back in their home so there was no time for my problems.

I had my phone off mute and the volume turned all the way up. It was no farther than five feet from me at all times on the job site. As you can imagine, the day dragged. Every minute felt like an hour. Were they going to call or what? My nerves were shot by 1 p.m. and I still had not heard anything at all. At 2 p.m., I thought, *Screw it. I obviously did not get the job.* Around 2:30 p.m. my partner asked me if I heard anything yet. I said, "No, not yet. They said they would call me, so let's hope they don't make me wait another week." Like clockwork, at 2:35 p.m., my phone started to ring. It's them. I answered the phone and I prepared myself for the bad news.

"So do you still want the job?" the producer asked.

"Um, yeah! I'm in, let's do it!" I said.

After about twenty minutes of all the formalities, I asked, "When do I start?"

"I'm thinking in a month or at least a few weeks or so," said the producer. Remember, this is almost 3 p.m. on Monday afternoon. "You fly out to Florida on Sunday afternoon." Whoa! Hit the brakes there, buttercup!

"Did you say this Sunday, like six days from now Sunday?" I asked.

"Yep."

They were already three weeks behind schedule with getting me hired so my first time out would be for four weeks because they need to catch up on filming. I told them that sounded good, but in the back of my mind, I was in full panic mode. They told me they'd have a contract to me later that day, I needed to get a physical and send the results to them before the weekend, and they'd see me in Jacksonville on Sunday. I was in full panic mode. We are in the final stages of rebuilding a house at work. I had a wife and kids and a business. I had less than a week to get my entire life together and head out for my first run that was going to be a month long.

My business partner was very understanding, and I thank him to this very day for that. After kicking butt for the rest of the week and getting the tree cut up in the backyard, Sunday arrived and I was heading out on a new adventure. I had no idea what to expect or what I was even doing, but I did know one thing: I was going to be a part of the biggest paranormal show in TV history.

I sadly had to leave the podcast at that point, but I left it in good hands and it ran for another year until my co-hosts decided they wanted to pursue other passions. My time there was amazing, and I owe that show a lot helping me through some dark times in my life and helping me make some lifetime friends. To this day, when I am doing appearances at paranormal conventions and events, I often get asked about the *American Ghost Hunter* show and if it will ever come back. It always makes me smile to know the fan base we had with that little podcast led to and opened so many doors for me.

Fast-forward to 2020 when I became co-owner of Paranormal Warehouse. In two years, we took the company from just a streaming service to a full-time working company that creates paranormal content and also produces ad content for major companies around the world. We have produced series such as *Epic Haunts*, the *Missing Reels*, and *Dead Live* to name just a few. So now you know why and how I got started in the paranormal field and why I am so passionate about it.

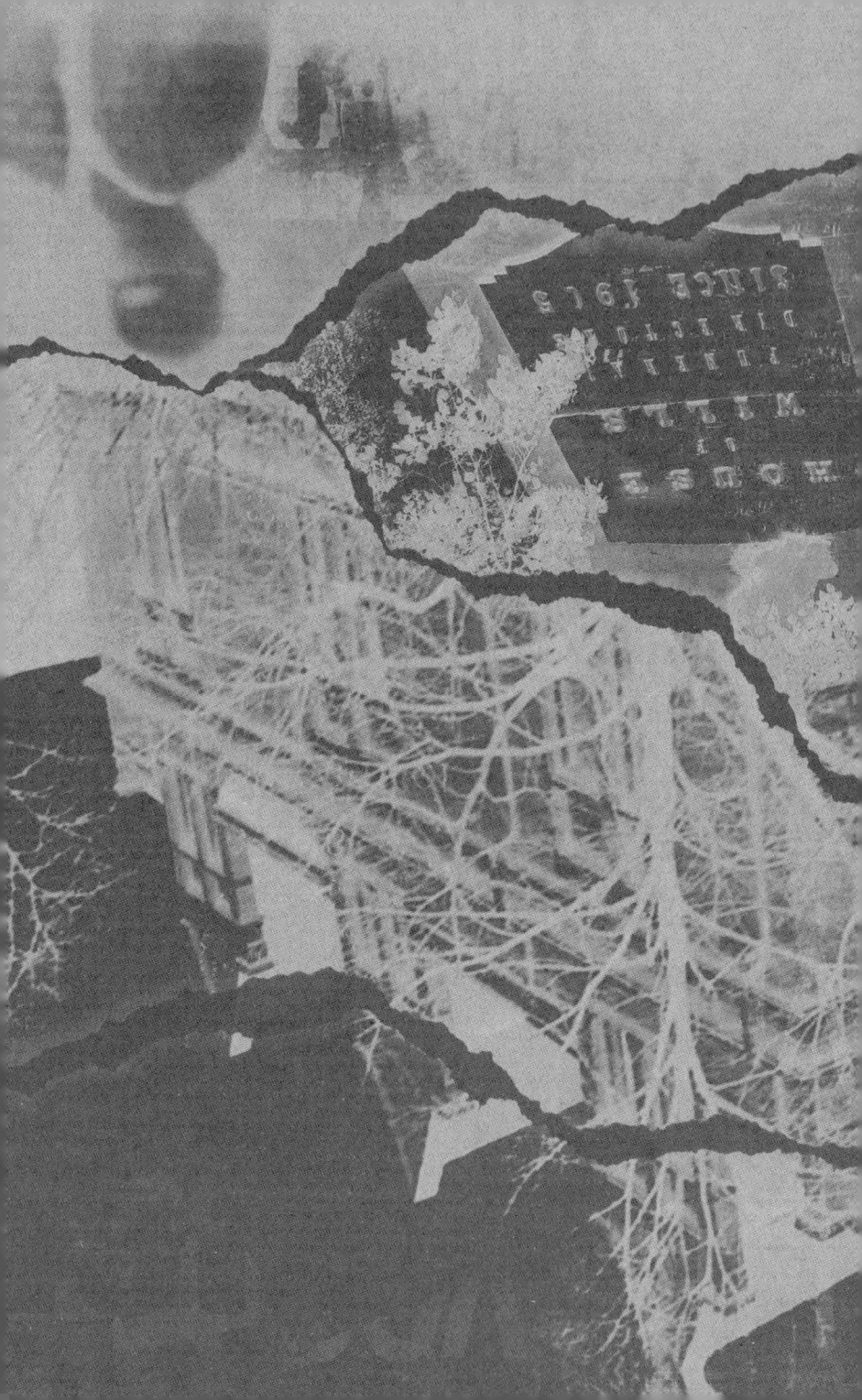

Chapter 16

The Reckoning

When I finally sat down to write this book, I was torn on how to tell this story and rehash all those memories from my time spent at the House of Wills. It took me almost seven years to finally feel comfortable enough to do so, but I came to a point where I believed it was time to put it out there, especially after telling the shorter version of it for so many years in interviews and in conversations. My perspective of what happened shook me to the core for many years. Writing this book was almost like therapy for me. I know for most paranormal investigators, this type of thing doesn't happen and for them it seems like fiction. Believe me, I thought the same thing before it happened to me, and it changed my perspective on many things in life, including the paranormal. I learned more about the paranormal from this one investigation than I did from all the years investigating combined. That's why the House of Wills is always the investigation that has come up so many times in my life. It's as if I'm to be haunted by it for the remainder of my life. That place changed me as an investigator, and as a man it tore me down and humbled me in so many ways. It almost beat me at one point, and I was on the brink of quitting my passion for investigating the paranormal. But somehow, I pulled out of it and recreated myself and changed my ways of investigating. I began to see things differently. My views changed on how I looked at certain aspects of the paranormal. I changed the way I investigated and became more grounded so the sort of effects I had from the House of Wills would never happen to me again.

These days, I go into all my investigations as a complete observer. I am only there to collect evidence and not to act as some paranormal celebrity trying to get a rise out of whatever or whoever is there.

I've learned a whole new level of respect for what I do in the field of the paranormal. I have surrounded myself with like-minded people who have a lot of the same views and level of respect for the dead as I do. Because of this, I have made progress that I never knew was possible and have learned so much more about this field that we really don't know that much about to begin with. Having said that, I also know the entertainment side of it all and I understand that not all people want to grow as investigators. Some people just like being scared and love the classic jump scare whether it's proven paranormal activity or not. This is where I personally separate the phrases "ghost hunter" and "paranormal investigator." I might catch a little flack for this, but this is my opinion only. A ghost hunter is someone who likes going out on some designated weekend with friends to a local haunted house or graveyard and gets random spirit responses on a piece of equipment. A paranormal investigator wants to investigate known haunted locations with documented backstories, uses scientific equipment and experiments, and opens their evidence to others to be scrutinized by the public and by peers in the community. I know all of this coming from being the co-lead investigator on *Ghost Hunters*. I embrace and understand both sides of this field.

My feelings on the House of Wills are mixed these days. I almost feel as if I was too harsh in speaking of it the way I have in the past. The location to me is one of a living entity, much like a predator in the wild such as a shark or a wolf. It is just doing what comes natural to it by feeding on the weak. Something I have learned and come to grips with since my time there is that good does not exist without evil and vice versa. This is all part of the circle of life in a way. The building is only doing what it does best by creating havoc and feeding off all the negative energy around it. This is no different from what some of us do as humans. We feed off good and bad energy that is around us all the time and, in a lot of ways, controls the outcome of our everyday life. We all know that one person that we encounter almost daily who is always negative and nothing makes them happy. On the other hand, you have that other person where no matter how bad things are, they are always happy and find the silver lining in everything bad or good in their lives. The type of people and energy you let into your life will shape the energy of your life. I decided several years ago to cut out all the negative people who were holding me back and concentrate on the positives in my life. It has made me a much happier person and a more successful one. We all have our bad days, but positive light and thinking will take you far away from it, rather than dwelling on it and letting it eat away at you.

These days I am in a much better place mentally and physically. I have educated myself enough about these types of hauntings to make myself more aware of my surroundings and to help others in these types of circumstances. This does not make me an expert by any means but only that I know enough to recognize what I need to look out for and how to protect myself and others.

Almost seven years later, I still have strange occurrences happen. Anytime I was writing the book or mentioned the name the House of Wills out loud, weird things would happen. Nothing too crazy, but things like strange smells or sounds that could not be accounted for in my house or the dog acting strangely. I was on a live stream show about eight months before I started writing this book. It was the host, two co-hosts, and myself. They asked, "What's the craziest place you have been?" I always break that down into two categories: on the show and off. I tell them on the show it is a toss-up between Clifton, Arizona, and Haines, Alaska. Off the show, I tell them it's definitely the House of Wills. One time when I mentioned its name off the show, a picture that had been hanging on my wall for the last five years fell off the wall and knocked over all my tripods. It scared all of us, even though my co-hosts were not in the room like I was. We all had quite the laugh about that, but that is an example of the things that happen when I mention the House of Wills. I think that's why it took me so long to write this book, because in all honesty, I didn't want to relive it. I wrote this book to basically get it off my chest and put it out there. Not because people have been asking me to write it or I felt pressured into it in any way. But now that I have, I feel so much better and stronger for it.

Chapter 17

Reflection

I look back at everything that has happened to me since this one night spent in the House of Wills, and I honestly believe that one night changed my life's course of direction. I was able to be a part of a hit TV show seen around the world by millions of people. It's allowed me to turn my hobby and passion into a full-time job where I travel to places around the country and do appearances several times a month and get to investigate haunted locations I would never have been able to before all of this. I have met so many interesting, amazing people, and all of them, in some way, have touched my life. They all hold a special place within me that will always be there. These are the memories that make me a wealthy man and that can never be taken from me. In some ways, I can say that the House of Wills has made me who I am today, but I cannot give it that kind of credit because I know what the location stands for and I will not sell myself or my soul for it. I will give it the credit it deserves by saying it helped educate me in my journey as a paranormal investigator and made me more aware of the darker side of the paranormal. It also taught me that true evil does exist, not only in the hearts of men but in the spirit world as well.

The emotions I feel these days about the spirit realm are much broader than before. My mind is more open, and I have removed the blinders that once held me back from seeing the truths of many things in life and in the paranormal. I can read people and my surroundings much better because of it. I'm not sure if it is due to my experiences over the last several years or old age setting in. I left a part of myself there and brought a part of it back with me. I will carry it around for the rest of my life. Knowing what I know now, I ask myself if I would I go back. Honestly, I have to say yes. I feel that the House of Wills and I have unfinished business and I need to try to come to complete peace with it someway or somehow.

Therefore, I try my best not to judge anyone who loves this field and whatever they believe when it comes to investigating. We all got into investigating or ghost hunting for our own reasons, whether it was the loss of a loved one, scientific reasons, or just to have fun and get scared at your local haunted house. It doesn't matter to me as long as we all have mutual respect for one another and we remember this is a pseudoscience. For us to further this field, we all need to stick together and push forward as a team with respect for one another and the spirits we are trying to communicate with. They were once living and breathing human beings like us. Remember this the next time you are investigating and you catch yourself asking those interrogating harsh questions and wonder why you are not getting any responses in return. We have all done it, especially when we first start out investigating. All I ask anyone reading this is to try not to make the same mistakes I have made in this field, especially when it comes to a location like the House of Wills. These types of places can not only mentally hurt you but also physically. They are not to be taken lightly, and thank God they are not as prevalent as some TV shows would make them out to seem.

I do know that if I ever return to the House of Wills, it will take a lot of convincing on my part to my family, especially after they read this book and know what that place is capable of. I think at this point in my life, my family's well-being and peace of mind are the only things that matter and would keep me from going back.

In 2019 while filming an episode of *Ghost Hunters*, I was staying in a hotel about twelve blocks away from the building. I tried convincing some of the production guys into going over and checking out the location, but with a tight filming schedule that week, it wasn't possible. Plus, they were very hesitant about going because two of them had already been there several years before with another TV show. Both the director of photography and the coordinating producer had very negative experiences there and refused to go back. Russ, our coordinating producer, stood about six foot three and weighed about two hundred and ninety pounds. I believe he could stop a runaway truck dead in its tracks if he wanted to, but he would not go back in that building. He could never explain the reason why, just that it messed with his head when he was there and that it stuck with him for a long time after. That was the closest I have been to the building in years, and I could literally feel it calling my name the whole week I was in Cleveland.

Who knows what the future holds for the House of Wills and for Eric. I can only hope the best for him and his endeavor to restore the building back to its original glory. I believe Eric has the best intentions for the property and for East Cleveland. I know him to be a hard-working businessman with a vision for the building. I also think Eric has somewhat fallen for the building like no one else has. It has its hooks in him, and he has become a victim of the slow burn. I believe his duty to the property is not so much in the role of its owner but more like a steward to its needs. House of Wills needs him to keep it alive and standing for many years to come. I believe no one will ever fully own that property because it owns itself and can never be tamed by man.

I do believe someday I will return to the House of Wills and further my investigation there and face down whatever it was that took a piece of me that night. I know better now what I am up against, and I will not be blindsided again like some unwilling participant who doesn't see it coming. This time I am ready for it and will be waiting for it to strike. I will not be beaten by this darkness that resides in the deep-est bowels of the building. I know it is still there and I have spoken to other victims that have fallen prey to it since my time there. It has nowhere to go. That place is its home and it feeds there every chance it gets. It's just sitting in wait for its next crop of victims to cross over the threshold into its lair.

Conclusion

As of February 28, 2022, I have been writing this book for the better part of a year now. I promised myself and others that I would probably never go back to the House of Wills for obvious reasons. It looks as if I will be breaking that promise to the people I love and myself at this point. It so happens that I have been asked to film a new show called *Dead Live* and the first location we are filming at is the House of Wills. It's funny in a way because this location was not supposed to be a part of the filming of the show. However, our first location fell through due to technical difficulties with filming there. Now, this is nothing new when filming a show. Locations fall through all the time due to one thing or another. I have had entire episodes that have taken a week to film and hundreds of hours of production never aire on television because of technical or legal reasons. But it so happens this location was the one that came up to fill in the void for the first episode. Maybe it's just all meant to be at this point. I hope that by the time this book is released, I will have already filmed there, as we are planning to film during the summer or fall of 2023. I do believe this time around I am better prepared for what may happen and that I have a better perspective on how to protect myself and the others around me while being there. It will be interesting to see what occurs this time around and to see if we get the same results that I had seven years ago. Until then, thank you all for your support and God bless all of us.

House of Wills
Floor Plans

Plan View: Roof

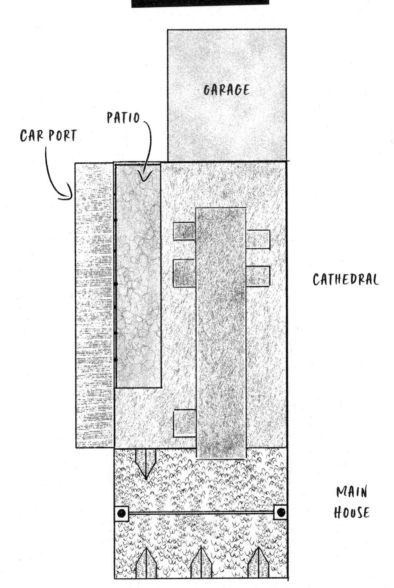

GARAGE

PATIO

CAR PORT

CATHEDRAL

MAIN
HOUSE

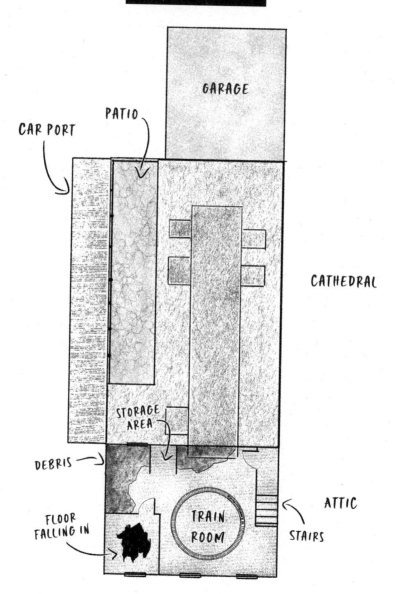

Plan View: Attic

GARAGE

CAR PORT

PATIO

CATHEDRAL

STORAGE AREA

DEBRIS

FLOOR FALLING IN

TRAIN ROOM

ATTIC

STAIRS

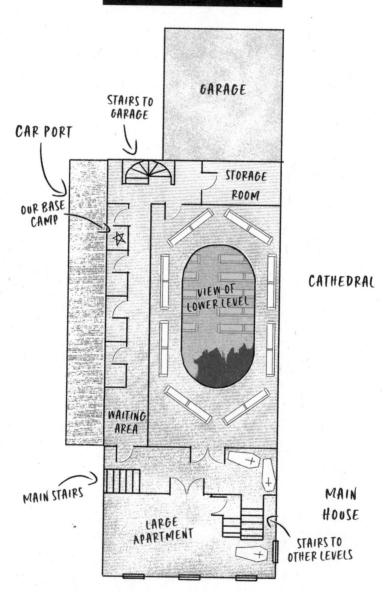

Plan View: 2nd Floor

GARAGE

STAIRS TO GARAGE

CAR PORT

STORAGE ROOM

OUR BASE CAMP

CATHEDRAL

VIEW OF LOWER LEVEL

WAITING AREA

MAIN STAIRS

MAIN HOUSE

LARGE APARTMENT

STAIRS TO OTHER LEVELS

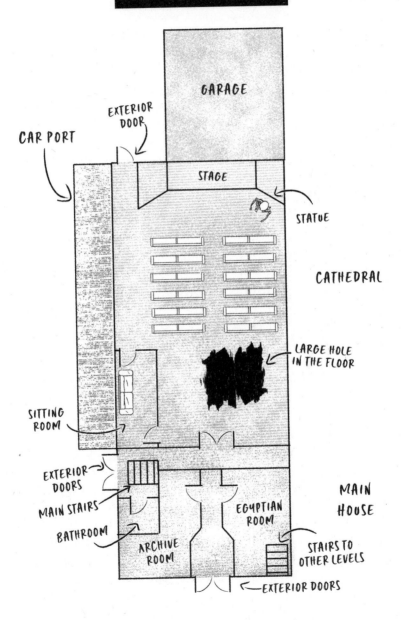

Plan View: 1st Floor

GARAGE

EXTERIOR DOOR

CAR PORT

STAGE

STATUE

CATHEDRAL

LARGE HOLE IN THE FLOOR

SITTING ROOM

EXTERIOR DOORS

MAIN STAIRS

BATHROOM

ARCHIVE ROOM

EGYPTIAN ROOM

MAIN HOUSE

STAIRS TO OTHER LEVELS

EXTERIOR DOORS

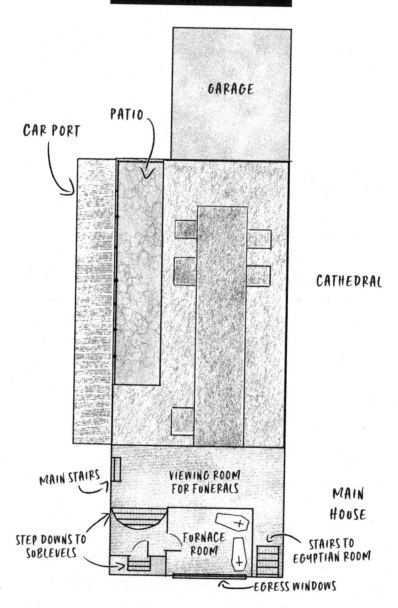

Plan View: Basement

GARAGE

PATIO

CAR PORT

CATHEDRAL

MAIN STAIRS

VIEWING ROOM
FOR FUNERALS

MAIN
HOUSE

STEP DOWNS TO
SUBLEVELS

FURNACE
ROOM

STAIRS TO
EGYPTIAN ROOM

EGRESS WINDOWS

To Write to the Author

If you wish to contact the author or would like more information about this book, please write to the author in care of Llewellyn Worldwide Ltd. and we will forward your request. Both the author and the publisher appreciate hearing from you and learning of your enjoyment of this book and how it has helped you. Llewellyn Worldwide Ltd. cannot guarantee that every letter written to the author can be answered, but all will be forwarded. Please write to:

Daryl Marston
℅ Llewellyn Worldwide
2143 Wooddale Drive
Woodbury, MN 55125-2989

Please enclose a self-addressed stamped envelope for reply, or $1.00 to cover costs. If outside the U.S.A., enclose an international postal reply coupon.

Many of Llewellyn's authors have websites with additional information and resources. For more information, please visit our website at http://www.llewellyn.com